Footprints
The Story Behind the Poem That Inspired Millions

by
Margaret Fishback Powers

HarperSanFrancisco
A Division of HarperCollinsPublishers

FOOTPRINTS: *The Story Behind the Poem That Inspired Millions.*
Copyright © 1993 by Margaret Fishback Powers.
All rights reserved. No part of this book may be used or reproduced
in any manner whatsoever without written permission
except in the case of brief quotations embodied in critical articles
and reviews. For information address HarperCollins Publishers,
10 East 53rd Street, New York, NY 10022.

HarperCollins books may be purchased for educational, business, or
sales promotional use. For information please write: Special Markets
Department, HarperCollins Publishers, Inc.,
10 East 53rd Street, New York, NY 10022.

HarperCollins Web Site: http://www.harpercollins.com

HarperCollins®, ■®, and HarperSanFrancisco™ are trademarks of
HarperCollins Publishers Inc.

FIRST HARPERCOLLINS PAPERBACK EDITION PUBLISHED 1998

ISBN 0–06–251557–8 (pbk.)

00 01 02 RRDH 10 9 8 7 6 5

Footprints

One night I dreamed a dream.
I was walking along the beach with my Lord.
Across the dark sky flashed scenes from my life.
For each scene, I noticed two sets of footprints in the sand,
one belonging to me and one to my Lord.
When the last scene of my life shot before me
I looked back at the footprints in the sand
and to my surprise,
I noticed that many times along the path of my life
there was only one set of footprints.
I realized that this was at the lowest
and saddest times of my life.
This always bothered me
and I questioned the Lord
about my dilemma.
'Lord, you told me when I decided to follow You,
You would walk and talk with me all the way.
But I'm aware that during the most troublesome
times of my life there is only one set of footprints.
I just don't understand why, when I needed You most,
You leave me.'
He whispered, 'My precious child,
I love you and will never leave you
never, ever, during your trials and testings.
When you saw only one set of footprints
it was then that I carried you.'

To my mom, Edith Elma Fishback, and the sweet memory of my dad, Clarence Henry Fishback.

Acknowledgements

My thanks to Lillian White, my teacher, and her husband, Kenneth, both lifelong friends; Dr. Barry and Audrey Moore, friends and counselors over the years; Dr. Geoffrey Still, our mentor and confidant throughout our marriage years, and his wife, Beverly, and their family; Dr. Thomas and Susan Standlee and their family, for unconditional friendship; Jeannette Clift George, actress, supporter, and lifelong friend; Fred and Elaine Burnett and Alma Frederick, and Norman and Florence DeRosiers, special friends, our homes away from home; Rev. John Ballard, for encouraging and promoting my work; Uncle Redd Harper, actor and singer, deceased February 1992; William Hendley, missionary, who was present on the "Footprints" weekend; my husband, Paul, and dearest daughters, Christina Michelle and Paula Margaret.

Special acknowledgements to Helen Hosier, ghostwriter (Texas); Helen Jenkins, proofreader (Calgary); Gena Gorrell, editor (Toronto); the Kelly family (Toronto); and Claude Primeau and Nancy Colbert at HarperCollins Publishers (Toronto).

Chapter One

Triple Trouble

> . . . but those who hope in the Lord
> will renew their strength.
> They will soar on wings like eagles;
> they will run and not grow weary,
> they will walk and not be faint. . . .
>
> Isaiah 40:31

"Oh, it's always so good to be home." I sighed as I said this, looking at Paul, my husband, who was stretched out relaxing. We'd been woken up early by the birds outside our window.

"Make the most of it, Margie," he responded, "we'll be off again tomorrow."

"Where to this time?" I asked, weariness sounding in my voice.

"Vancouver. . . ."

We'd just returned from a two-month series of church camps in Washington State. Summer was always our busiest season. Our "Little People's Ministry," which was dedicated to evangelism—to equipping and encouraging children to learn and grow spiritually—found us hopping from one camp, church, and crusade to another. Not that it wasn't challenging and fulfilling—of course it was, in fact it was one of the dreams of our lives come true—but toward the middle of the summer we were more than ready to kick back and relax at our home in Coquitlam, British Columbia.

Now it was August. As I looked at our travel itinerary, observing the date—Monday, August 7, 1989, a Canadian holiday—I thought we would at least sleep in. I didn't know it at the time, but the date was to be forever imprinted on our memories—an unforgettable day with triple events that would sear us for life.

Very early that Monday morning the phone rang. "I'll get it, stay put," I said to my husband.

"Hi Mom, how's everything?"

"It's Paula." I mouthed the words to Paul. "Everything's fine," I assured our daughter, "but we were just saying how good it felt to be home."

"Wellll . . . in that case, maybe I shouldn't ask," and she paused. But she knew her parents and what pushovers we are for kids, so it was only a momentary pause. "How would you like to drive a carload of kids up to Golden Ears and picnic at the Lower Falls?" Golden Ears was a vast provincial park, about ten miles away. "I need an extra vehicle, someone dropped out." She paused briefly again. "If you'll do it, the sooner you can come and meet us at the church, the better. Everyone's waiting. They're anxious to get this show on the road."

I glanced at Paul. "Okay, we'll come," I promised. I already knew what his reaction would be. There just wasn't anything he wouldn't do for kids; his own childhood had been so traumatic.

"Come just as you are," she said, and I could tell she was relieved. "Thanks, Mom, I knew I could count on you and Dad. Bring your swimsuit and wear your shorts."

I quickly pulled on my swimsuit, slipped some shorts on over it, and reached for the top I'd worn the day before. "I'll leave all this stuff behind," I said, remembering everything in the pockets.

"No, don't take time to clean out your pockets," Paul said. A few minutes later we were on our way out the door. As we drove the short distance to the church where Paula and the kids were waiting, I felt in the pockets of the shirt jacket, fingering the bottle of Paul's heart pills and another bottle of Extra-strength Tylenol. To myself I thought: *Why do I always load myself down with this stuff!*

We did a quick drive through McDonalds on our way out of town, the back of the van filled with kids. "Golden Ears Park, here we come," one of the kids shouted, and we all laughed. It was going to be a fun day. We enjoyed being with Paula and her young charges. We often jokingly said to each other and our friends that our daughters, Tina and Paula, and their young friends, kept us on our toes. There's no time to think about advancing years when you're around young people.

"What a gorgeous day," I said. Everyone agreed that they'd picked the right day. Twice before, the outing had been canceled due to inclement weather—B.C.'s liquid sunshine.

Upon arrival, we joined the others clambering out of cars. A few instructions to the group from Paula about the need to be careful—the rocks would be slippery and we'd be crossing the top of Lower Falls on a rock ledge—and we all took off. Just before leaving, Paula explained, "Now listen, you guys, there's a forty-foot-deep glacier pool off one side. No funny stuff, okay?"

We were proud of our beautiful daughter. She had such a love for young people, and she and her sister had always been a part of our work with youth. They were extremely gifted ventriloquists, and it was a delight to be around them. Now, as I watched her lead the kids, I saw her long strawberry-blonde hair swinging free as we approached the rock ledge walkway.

We all made our way cautiously across the slippery rocks, and found perches for ourselves on the rocks as we paused to rest and enjoy the breathtakingly beautiful scenery. We watched rather anxiously as some older fellows (not part of our group) dove into the glacier pool from high atop a rock perch. "That water is ice-cold," I called to Paula. "How can they stand it!"

"I don't know," she called back, shaking her head, "I'm glad it's not me!"

Paul elected to stay on the other side of the glacier pool, where there was another smaller pocket of water that looked inviting. He had said to me, "This is where I'm going to read." I knew he wanted to prepare for the Vancouver meetings. He carefully made his way around to where he could enjoy the beauty and have some seclusion.

We saw lots of swimmers and sunbathers enjoying themselves on the rocks and in the water. Looking down, we could see others amusing themselves at the base of the falls and in the river. I couldn't help thinking that there should be barricades or fences, and signs warning people that it was dangerous and slippery in places.

"It's so beautiful up here," one of the girls remarked.

"Absolutely heavenly," I chimed in, thinking to myself that it felt as if we were so close to heaven that we could almost reach up and touch God. Spruce and pine trees towered above us with the sun filtering through. The glacier water was emerald-green.

After sunning awhile, I looked at my watch and called across to my husband, "Paul, it's 2:15." Paul glanced up from his reading and acknowledged that he'd heard me.

Just then, Paula said, "I'm going back across to where Dad is." She started out over the rock ledge. At the same time, somewhere nearby, a dog barked, startling me.

As a mother, I thought about the sixty-eight-foot falls on the one side and the forty-foot-deep glacier pool on the other, and called out, cautioning her, "Oh, be careful!" I watched as she inched her way along. Paul was also watching as she made her way. He stood up and held out his hand to reach for her when she got closer. At that moment she missed her footing and suddenly fell into a whirlpool of water. It sucked her into its vortex, spinning her around three times, and before any of us knew what was happening, she was spun out and over the falls.

Everyone was screaming. I jumped to my feet, screaming too. I couldn't help Paula, what should I do? Just then, I glanced across at my husband and saw him clutch his chest and fall. At that moment, I knew he was having a heart attack—I could actually see his color change. It was all happening as if in slow motion, but the confusion was terrible and I feared for the lives of the other young people if they should panic. I turned my back momentarily to face the kids, who were hysterical. "We must pray," I shouted, crying out, "Oh God, help us!"

I reached for a necklace I had around my neck that Paul had given me on our twenty-third wedding anniversary, just the year before. I glanced down at the eagle mounted on black onyx and sent a telegram-prayer heavenward: "Lord, if You are going to take Paula, take her without too much pain, and oh dear God, spare my husband."

I thought my daughter must surely be dead. How could anyone survive a sixty-eight-foot fall into glacier-cold water? I knew I had to get to my husband, but I instinctively also knew I couldn't trust my shaky legs to the slippery rock ledge. Just as I was about to enter the water to swim across, a voice called to me from where my husband was. "I'm going to throw this rope across the pool. My son is alongside you, he'll grab it. Hang onto the rope as you swim across."

What I didn't know was that the man's wife was a nurse who was at that very moment administering aid to Paul. Earlier that day, as they left their home, the man had grabbed the rope which they used to tether their dog, and his son had said to him, "What are you doing with that rope?"

"I don't know," he'd replied, as he stuck it in his pocket. Now I was holding onto the rope with one hand as I swam with the other hand. The water was icy cold but I was oblivious of it as I made my way across.

Down below, some boys on the rocks at the base of the falls saw a body floating by and, thinking it was a corpse, pulled it ashore. A woman sunning on the rocks observed all this, rushed over, and immediately began resuscitation. I found out later that this woman was a nurse trained specifically in drowning accidents.

I struggled onto the rocks, anxious to reach my husband's side, with the man who had been holding the rope helping me. But somehow, in my desperate and frantic attempt, I slipped several times on the slimy rocks and broke my right arm. It hung limp at my side and as soon as I was out of the water I was aware of excruciating pain. Then I saw a woman bending over Paul. The man told me, "She's a nurse, trained in cardiac arrest."

"Thank God," I murmured, my whole body shaking uncontrollably. Suddenly I remembered and told the nurse that in my left pocket was a bottle of Nitrol heart medicine. Someone noticed me trembling and thoughtfully threw a large towel around me.

At one point, the nurse turned and calmly said, "They tell me that's your daughter who went over the falls. My sister-in-law is down below, she's a nurse trained in water rescue."

I fell back on the rocks, overcome with emotion, grateful to think that perhaps Paula had been rescued.

I was just beginning to pass out when I heard the nurse add, "Oh, it's too bad we don't have some pain medicine." I tried reaching into my right pocket, but could only motion.

"She's a walking pharmacy," she said, as she found the bottle of Extra-strength Tylenol.

The presence of both these nurses was amazing, but they explained that they were on strike in our provincial hospitals, which was why they were there on an outing. One of the swimmers we'd seen diving was also a long-distance runner. He immediately took off, running to reach the nearest phone and call in ambulances for help. Somehow the kids all carefully made their way back to the cars, waiting prayerfully while anxiously wondering what was to be the outcome of all this.

A search-and-rescue team arrived first, and were already starting to carry us out when the ambulances came. Stretchers were then brought in. Four hours after the accidents, we were in emergency rooms at Maple Ridge Hospital. At three in the morning I learned that X-rays had revealed that Paula had a broken neck, her arm had been pulled out of its socket, and she had a perforated kidney and liver. She was a gravely injured young woman, but she was alive.

Nearby, in the intensive care ward, my husband lay hooked to heart monitors and intravenous tubes. Early in the morning a nurse came and asked him,

"Mr. Powers, would you like me to pray for you, your daughter, and your wife?" He nodded yes, and then she prayed.

When she finished praying, she said, "I think it would help you if I read a little piece I have here in my pocket," and she pulled out a card. Holding my husband's hand, she quietly read:

> One night I dreamed a dream.
> I was walking along the beach with my Lord.
> Across the dark sky flashed scenes from my life.
> For each scene, I noticed two sets
> of footprints in the sand,
> one belonging to me
> and one to my Lord.
> When the last scene of my life shot before me
> I looked back at the footprints in the sand.
> There was only one set of footprints.
> I realized that this was at the lowest
> and saddest times of my life.
> This always bothered me
> and I questioned the Lord
> about my dilemma.
> "Lord, you told me when I decided to follow You,
> You would walk and talk with me all the way.
> But I'm aware that during the most troublesome
> times of my life there is only one set of footprints.
> I just don't understand why, when I needed You most,
> You leave me."
> He whispered, "My precious child,
> I love you and will never leave you
> never, ever, during your trials and testings.
> When you saw only one set of footprints
> it was then that I carried you."

When the nurse finished reading, she looked at my husband and said, "I don't know the author, it's anonymous."

Paul lifted his hand very weakly and said, "I do, I know the author." The nurse thought he wasn't fully conscious because of the medication he'd been given, but Paul said again, "I know the author very well . . . it's my wife."

Chapter Two

Encounter with Destiny

"Across the dark sky flashed scenes from my life. . . ."

With my husband and daughter in hospital beds, both in intensive care, and with my arm in a cast, the landscape of our lives seemed overshadowed by a dark sky. Yet Paul and Paula were alive, miraculously so, and I knew from past experience that during this troublesome time we would be carried. God had carried us before; He would carry us now.

Paul told me about the nurse reading the "Footprints" poem. We were both overwhelmed to think that something I'd written in 1964 was now speaking so much comfort to our hearts, more than twenty years later. My mind reached back to embrace treasured memories as I reflected on our lives.

I remembered my first two meetings with Paul Powers. The second time, his jeans were dirty—in fact, his clothes were cobwebby. Not exactly a picture of the well-groomed, dignified, irresistible Prince Charming every girl dreams of riding off with into the future! I was living in the High Park area of Toronto, and my younger brother Jim had asked me to accompany him to a bookstore. While we were there, we bumped into Paul, who was working in the bookstore. "Hey, great to see you," Paul and Jim both exclaimed as they slapped each other on the shoulders.

"Oh, these are my sisters, Margie and Ruby," Jim added, offhandedly introducing us. "I think you may have met once, three or four years ago, out at the farm. Girls, this is Paul Powers. We were buddies in high school."

I couldn't tell if Paul remembered me from that first meeting, but I remembered him. In fact, I remembered that occasion distinctly, because he was in and out quite fast that day and I'd said to my mother, "That's one guy I wouldn't marry if he was the last man on earth!"

I wouldn't have admitted it at the time, but I was probably miffed because he didn't pay more attention to me. My mother came to his defense. "He's delivering a film for our high-school Bible Club, and he doesn't have time to spare. He just wanted to say a quick hello to Jim. He's on his way to a Youth for Christ rally in Simcoe." I remembered that Jim had said Paul was attending the London College of Bible and Mission.

Now we were face to face again and I was sizing him up. He was about twenty-five—four years older than I was. Behind his dark-rimmed glasses I couldn't help but notice blue-gray eyes that fairly danced. In spite of his grubby appearance, he was good-looking with his dark hair and suntanned face.

He apologized for his dirty clothes. "I'm moving things around," he said, wiping his perspiring face.

It was a hot August afternoon and I was suddenly conscious of my own appearance, wondering how *I* looked. His gaze was so penetrating. He had a book in his hands and he extended it to me as he said, "Are you married?"

I looked at the title and read *How to Have a Happy Marriage.* His question caught me by surprise, as he no doubt knew it would. Did I detect a smile on his face? The incident made me upset and I quickly retorted, "No, and I don't plan to get married, either!" I was really short with him. Today he would tell you that I "barbed" at him and that I "clipped" him, intending to set him in his place. I softened my response somewhat, however, by asking him, "Are you married?"

He grinned and replied, "No, but I'm sure thinking about it."

What Paul didn't know was that I was still getting over a relationship that had broken up, and I wasn't thinking too kindly about *any* man at that point.

"You know, I think we all need a cool drink," Paul said. "Let's go downstairs to the Honeydew Restaurant." I was a bit reluctant, but Ruby and Jim thought it was a great idea. "Their specialty is this fantastic honeydew drink—honey, orange juice, milk, and some honeydew melon juice," Paul explained. The drink was refreshing, and so was the conversation. Paul was a delightful conversationalist and had us all laughing.

"What brings you to Toronto?" Paul asked me.

"I'm taking some summer-school classes in connection with my work as a teacher," I replied. I'd been teaching for three years; Ruby was still in high school.

"And I'm helping Jim with his work." I didn't tell him then what Jim's work was.

"By the way, Paul," Jim said, "we're going to the Exhibition on Saturday." The Canadian National Exhibition was an annual treat for us, with its displays and contests and exciting atmosphere. "Have you been yet?"

"No," he replied, "but I'd like to go. I can get Saturday off. Margie, mind if I come along? I'd like to take you."

A date? I fumbled for an excuse. There *was* something sweet about this fellow, even if he was a tad earnest. *You need some fun,* I rationalized. But that would be it. Just some time out for fun. "You'll never regret saying yes," Paul promised, the excitement in his eyes nearly convincing me I wouldn't.

That's how it happened that I spent the following Saturday with this fellow whose conversation was so refreshing. After Paul finally located us at the funeral parlor where my brother worked and stayed, we were on our way. "You didn't tell me you lived in a mortuary," Paul quipped. "I've been searching for this place for a while." The way he said it, it became a big joke. At first, though, I thought he'd changed his mind.

It had rained earlier and the drenching downpour had turned the Exhibition parking lot into a bog. Paul got out of the car, sloshed over to the passenger side, and saw me hesitate, my feet dangling over a muddy puddle. In an instant, he reached inside the car, saying, "Here, let me lift you out," as he swept me up in his strong arms, depositing me safely beyond the puddle.

As we walked along, I slipped and almost fell. Paul grabbed my arm. "You're so tiny," he said, "I'm going to have to carry you or we'll lose you in one of these puddles!" We laughed. But I didn't think it was so funny when we reached the turnstiles and the gatekeeper charged him for one adult and one child. It didn't help when Paul corrected the man and he looked flustered and said, "Oh, I thought she was your daughter." I'd been mistaken for a child before, being under five feet tall, so I took it as a good sport, but I suddenly knew I didn't want to be mistaken for Paul Powers' daughter.

The wide-striped exposition tents billowed in the wind, and the Ferris wheel and the many other rides packed with merrymakers jostling one another added to the carnival atmosphere. The music all but drowned out our conversation.

Neither of us really cared for the rides, but we tried a few. We enjoyed the home shows and displays more than anything, and there we could talk and hear each other. We quickly found ourselves talking about every subject imaginable—the things we enjoyed, such as music and good books, and other mutual interests.

At one point we found a more secluded place to rest and he asked about my work as a missionary teacher in Maniwaki, Quebec, and the class of Indian-, French-, and English-speaking children I'd been teaching in the first three grades of school. "Illness forced me to give that up," I explained. "It broke my heart. But I'll be teaching near Tillsonburg this fall."

Paul was very kind as he expressed concern. "May I ask what happened?"

"There was an electrical storm," I said slowly, remembering with pain the events of May 1963. "Lightning flashed from mountain peak to mountain peak, alarming some of the students, but most were accustomed to the daytime storms. I had always cautioned my pupils to keep the windows closed during storms like that. However, Jimmie, one of the students, opened the window 'only a wee crack,' as he said, to get a breath of fresh air. Poor Jimmie suffers from cerebral palsy."

I looked into Paul's face. It showed such interest that I continued. "A bolt of lightning flashed through the open window as I stood at the blackboard writing lessons, and sparks flew from the ends of my fingers. I was thrown down, and came to my senses on the floor against the side wall of the classroom. Weakly, I picked myself up, dusting myself off and apologizing as best I could to the children, and then went back to the lessons.

"But the electrical shock made me very dizzy and ill. As the day progressed, the milk chart and attendance sheet jumped up and down before my bleary eyes. That afternoon I dismissed the class early and cradled my head in my arms on the desk. The pain was almost unbearable. In the days that followed, I became increasingly ill, and the pain in my back and arm increased to the point where I was visibly shaking most of the time.

"Still, I worked that next week. But on Friday, when my best friend, Betty Reside, came to visit, she took one look at me and rushed me off to the hospital, where I remained for some time. My condition was much more serious than any of us had originally thought, and it was weeks before I was able to go home. The schoolboard officers were unable to renew my teaching contract, as I had no guarantee of complete recovery. That's when I came back home."

Paul had been very quiet through my lengthy explanation, but his grip on my hands was tender, yet strong, and this imparted strength to me. I felt so comfortable in his presence as his eyes searched mine. "God has been my strength, Paul," I confided, "and He has been carrying me through."

When we started talking about the Lord, we knew we were on the same wavelength. The more we shared events from our lives, the more comfortable we felt with each other. We discovered that we had a mutual concern to reach people and to impact their lives with the truths of God's Word. An initial bonding took place which had its roots in our desire to have our steps ordered by the Lord.

Paul would tell you that by the end of the day he was smitten, that he was "head over heels" in love with me and that I had "the right bait."

We had fun that Saturday at the Exhibition. Paul says that my "cat eyes" were sparkling by the end of the day, that he could tell I enjoyed life and having fun, but that there were some other hurts and bad experiences I hadn't shared with him that needed to be put behind me. He determined in his heart that he would help me to forget. I didn't know that he had a past that he was seeking to forget, with God's help—that, in fact, he was a victim of child abuse. There was much we needed to learn about each other, and we would in the days ahead. I felt inexplicably drawn to him.

My brother, sister, and I had accepted a dinner invitation for that evening, and we invited Paul along. It was the perfect climax to a wonderful day. Good fun and the beginning of a relationship that would go through lots of troublesome times. But we would have each other. More important, the two of us had the Lord walking with us.

That memorable Saturday evening, Jim offered to give Paul a lift back to his apartment. He and I sat together in the back seat, still talking. Just as Jim pulled up to Paul's door, he said, "Good night," and kissed me.

It surprised me, but not unpleasantly. "I had a really great time," I told him.

"Me too," he said. "How about if I write you?"

As we drove away, I told my brother, "He had a nice day, but he won't write." How wrong I was!

Chapter Three

Faltering Steps

"My precious child, I love you and will never leave you."

Sometimes nature gets angry in a very random and violent way. At any given moment around the world, there are more than a thousand storms, and oftentimes those storms give birth to lightning. And lightning can kill.

Scientists have found that one stroke of lightning produces more than 15 million volts. A spark between a cloud and the Earth may measure as much as eight miles long, traveling at a rate of 100 million feet per second. Lightning reaching between oppositely charged clouds may have a length of twenty miles.

Although I was a schoolteacher, I couldn't have told you these things; nor could I have told you that lightning kills more people (on average) per year than hurricanes and tornadoes combined. I didn't know that lightning blasts through the atmosphere at an estimated rate of two billion flashes a year. Lightning kills one person and injures four others every day in the United States alone. Yet the chances of being struck by lightning are about one in a million. The chances of being struck and surviving are even more remote. As one news reporter wrote: The chance of surviving a lightning strike is a roll of the dice.

I survived, but one of my students didn't. A great sadness invaded my young life that day I was struck by a flash of lightning as I stood before my class.

His name was Alfred. He was just a tiny boy, but he made a big impact on my life. Alfred introduced me to death in a way that I'd never been touched by it before.

Alfred had hardly spoken a word for the entire year, and now here it was May; the school year was almost over. I'd had the children make beautiful hexagonal baskets, and most of them had taken their baskets home at least a month before. When I asked Alfred why he delayed, he gently whispered that he was waiting for the right and special moment when his basket could be filled.

That afternoon, as I was feeling the effects of the electrical jolt, Alfred stood beside me, an angelic smile breaking over his face. "See this, teacher," he said, holding up the largest mass of yellow dandelions I had ever seen.

They were so healthy and pretty, I hated to cut the stems off to make them fit his little basket, but that's what he was asking me to do. He carefully placed them in his pretty basket, and then raced out the door to the waiting bus. I could still see him waving happily as he was boarding.

At that point, I collapsed into one of the student desks and thanked the Lord that some progress had been made with wee Alfred. He really could talk, after all!

Shortly after that, I left for my boarding house. I rested for a couple of hours, but the pain in my right arm had been steadily increasing since the shock of a few hours before. The electrical storm was now at its finest and fullest. I was glad to be inside where it was cozy, safe, and warm.

As I sat propped up in bed, trying to catch up on my French studies, I found it difficult to concentrate. Then the phone rang. I couldn't believe what I was hearing. My mind refused to comprehend it. "No, no, it can't be," I said, at the same time fighting the nausea that suddenly gripped me. But it was true.

My caller informed me that wee Alfred had been pushing his little sisters into the house when a bolt of lightning had struck him down. Although barely conscious, he had insisted that his parents allow him to take his little basket when they drove him to the hospital. He had died shortly after his arrival there.

The days that followed were extremely trying for me. It was with much difficulty that I assumed the teacher's role—attending the memorial service for this darling child and playing the organ. In the days that followed, I often found myself engulfed in tears. "Why Alfred? Why him? Why wasn't it me?" Questions. My mind replayed the last few moments I'd had with my student. He had been such a sweet and gentle little boy.

I began to think about death. Solemn thoughts for a young woman. I turned the pages of my Bible seeking help. It would become a habit of the heart—looking into God's Word for direction and for answers to my questions. I was not disappointed. In Jeremiah 1 :23 I found God speaking to an ancient prophet, telling him that our lives are not our own; that it is not for us to direct our steps.

It made me think. We want heaven populated with the elderly, not children or young people in what we feel is their prime of life. But Jesus loved the children when He was here on earth. He gathered them about Him, and told us to be like them. Of course He would want them in heaven also. I remembered Alfred's trusting ways, his quietness and kindness.

I found other verses in the Bible which assured me that death is not the end, that for those who love God and are His children through believing in His Son, Jesus, and accepting Him into their lives, eternal life in heaven is assured. Heaven is a prepared place for a prepared people.

I remembered Jesus' words to His disciples concerning heaven: "Do not let your hearts be troubled. Trust in God; trust also in me. In my Father's house are many rooms; if it were not so, I would have told you. I am going there to prepare a place for you" (John 14:1-4).

As I shared with my students my understanding about death and heaven, I discovered that they were accepting death in a beautiful, childlike, and peaceful manner. They were very subdued, and I think they missed their usually silent friend's presence. One wee girl assured me that death was like being carried home to heaven in Jesus' arms, where He would put us gently down to sleep on His big white pillow. Such an imagination! And such trust! She encouraged me, her teacher, never to be afraid, as God was always there. Later, her words were like an echo in the back of my mind as one day I wrote, "My precious child, I love you and will never leave you. . . ."

My students gave me much-needed comfort and strength throughout the next few days. I would need it even more in the days ahead. I wasn't able to finish out the rest of the school year, for immediately after that I was taken to the hospital, and the physical effects of the electrical shock were such that it took a few months before I began to recover. I had to give up my class and move home to my parents. I suffered extreme migraine headaches as a result of the shock, and during treatment my long curly auburn hair had to be cut. As it grew back, I was left with one giant patch of white which would remain with me throughout my life, a reminder always to be thankful for each day that God gives.

Recovering from the emotional effects took somewhat longer. During that period of my life, I discovered that some people cannot understand or accept death or illness. They search in the wrong places for answers to their questions. They become angry with God.

Although I didn't fully understand it at the time, in God's good providence, a relationship I thought was headed somewhere was terminated. If I had fought to hold onto the relationship, if I had made compromises, things might have turned out differently. But I could not give up my beliefs.

At the time, I felt it to be a very sad period. Certainly I overdramatized it in my mind—the poet in me was always seeking ways to express itself, and I was still quite young. I had some maturing to do, and heartaches are a part of the learning and growing process. Friends called me a hopeless romantic; now I only felt hopeless.

Slowly, however, while recuperating at our family farmhouse in Tillsonburg, I began to recognize that I needed to trust God fully with the events that came into my life.

Today I can confidently say that I know that anyone who does that can be sure that God is ordering not only our steps, but also our stops. And even when we feel we are walking a lonely, difficult, or sad path, we are not alone. His words ring true:

"My precious child,
I love you and will never leave you,
never, ever, during your trials and testings.
When you saw only one set of footprints
it was then that I carried you."

Chapter Four

Love Letters Straight from the Heart

As for God, his way is perfect. . . .

Psalm 18:30

The joy-filled Saturday with Paul Powers at the Canadian National Exhibition prompted a flood of thoughts in the days following. I thought through the events that had taken place since May and found, to my surprise and delight, that my perspective had changed considerably just since the encounter with Paul.

I even anticipated the daily trip to the mailbox, and was rewarded when, midway through the week, there was a letter from Toronto with Paul's return address. He had written to me that very Sunday, and now I held his letter in my hands. To say I was pleased and excited would be an understatement. Eagerly I found a quiet place where I would be undisturbed, and started reading.

Paul wrote another letter on Wednesday, which I received on Friday. His letters began to reveal things about him that I had only surmised—I had sensed his spiritual depth, but because our time together had been so short, I hadn't been quite able to fully grasp or appreciate it.

I was literally headed for the mailbox to send Paul a letter on Saturday when he showed up himself, with my brother. Jim had invited him to the farm for the weekend but hadn't called to let us know. I handed Paul my letter and once again he came up with one of his quips: "Personal delivery, no less!"

"It's great that you're here," I remember saying, trying not to sound too excited.

Paul immediately offered his services to my father, and Dad took him up on it. He cut the lawn—a half-acre, with our old push mower—and helped my father get rid of a hornets' nest under the eaves. I was out there pulling weeds, hoeing in the garden, raking up the grass—just so I could be near Paul, although I wouldn't have admitted it to anyone, not even to myself.

In the evening, we played Monopoly and popped corn. We had a wonderful time and we all got to know Paul better.

On Sunday we attended our church, the North Broadway Baptist Church, where Paul was reunited with a London Bible College friend, our pastor, Lambert Baptist. The rest of the day flew by all too fast and, before we knew it, Jim and Paul were headed back to Toronto. Paul promised to write some more and, busy as he was, he kept his word by writing two or three times weekly for the next several weeks. I wrote him lots of letters, too. Once I mailed three in a single day! I was revealing more about myself to him that I'd ever imagined wanting to. I told him things about myself I'd never told anyone. We really were becoming friends, close friends. And whenever he could, he'd come to the farm to visit.

"Tell me about your childhood," he said on one of those visits. "Have you always loved the piano?"

"You should ask my parents about that," I responded. "Oh, Paul, you won't believe it, but I actually composed music in my sleep. I was a sleepwalker when I was little, and in the middle of the night I'd get up, come downstairs, and sit at the piano. The rest of the family didn't much appreciate it," and we laughed.

"But in answer to your question, my parents sacrificed to get a piano for me. I started playing by ear at age six. My father used to turn on the radio, hear a song he liked, and say, 'Now Midge, hear that? I'll turn the radio off, and you play it on the piano,' and that's what I'd do. I wanted lessons, and people used to tell me that now I would never be able to learn from lessons. But I made up my mind that I'd prove them wrong. So at age thirteen I started learning properly."

"And today you're studying to be a composer and concert pianist," Paul said admiringly. "God has really gifted you, Marge."

I thanked him for his compliments, and told him that I appreciated his understanding that giftedness—whatever form it takes—is from God. "I want my poetry and music to always be an expression of what God has put into my heart and soul," I said, and I really meant it.

"They will, Margie," he said quietly, patting my hands, "they will. . . ," and there were tears in his eyes.

"Tell me about your childhood, Paul," I said.

He hesitated and then answered. "It bears no resemblance to your happy and carefree childhood, Margie. . . ."

It was then that I began to learn about Paul's past. I discovered things that, in the privacy of my own room, as I reflected on what Paul had told me, made me sob. I wept in Paul's presence, too; there was no way I could keep back the tears.

His mother died when he was still very young, and what followed can only be described as child abuse. As Dr. James Dobson said a few years ago, after interviewing Paul on his "Focus on the Family" radio program, "Paul Powers was one of the most pathetic victims of child abuse I have ever known. . . ."

Immediately following the death of his mother, as this terrified seven-year-old stood by, sobbing his little heart out, his drunken father struck him in the face with his fist, knocking him all the way across the room. But the beating didn't stop there. With blood streaming from Paul's nose and mouth, his father kicked and stomped on him, shouting, "For cryin' out loud! Shut up, you stupid kid. Real men don't cry, babies cry," as he continued kicking him in the side, the face, and everywhere.

The same ambulance that carried Paul's dead mother away also carried Paul to the hospital, where he spent several days being treated for a broken wrist, broken ribs, a badly swollen eye, lacerations, and several missing teeth. "But I didn't cry," Paul told me. "I vowed I'd never cry again."

Paul lost not only his mother that day, but also his childhood. He became a bitter little boy forced to be a "man" overnight, and in the process he paid a terrible price. He had a tragic childhood marred by the heavy drinking of his father, who was often in a drunken stupor, and then his father's remarriage, with more children being brought into the home by his step-mother, and yet more children being born in subsequent years. By the time he was eight he had been in and out of trouble with the police, as innocent child's play with neighborhood children turned into shoplifting, gang robbery, and eventually murder.

He spent years being bounced from one reform school to another, and finally did "hard time" in a prison that had formerly been a prisoner-of-war camp for captured German soldiers. By the time he was sixteen he was a hardened delinquent, and was taken to an even more secure prison in Guelph, Ontario, where he spent much of his time in solitary confinement. But it was there that he was given the chance to participate in a trade school which revealed his creative abilities. This eventually resulted in privileges being granted. He was transferred to Bowmanville and worked in a shoe factory, and the job was a turning-point. While he was on the work-release program he boarded with an elderly Christian couple, Clara and Clarence Adams, and his life changed dramatically.

"I was invited to a Youth for Christ meeting by a girl I'd been dating," he explained to me, "and I went—several times, in fact." His voice broke as he talked to me, and tears came into his eyes.

"You're crying," I said gently.

"Yes," he said, "I'd spent all those years locking things up, since my mother died, and the dam finally burst following one of those meetings. God and I had a good talk. I sought Jesus' forgiveness, like the thief on the cross, which I'd heard about the night before. God the Father whispered that He loved me, and I believed Him. Now I can cry and know it's okay. . . ."

In September 1959 he had moved to London, Ontario, to do Youth for Christ work in juvenile and family court, as well as in area rallies. He was now doing area rallies around Belleville, as well as counselling young offenders in the area—youths going through much of the turmoil he himself had suffered.

Whatever Paul didn't tell me that day soon found its way into his letters, as our weekly correspondence continued. Before long I knew these were love letters straight from his heart, and "I love you" began to surface.

Chapter Five

Reflections

Live as children of light . . .
and find out what pleases the Lord. . . .

Ephesians 5: 8

$\mathcal{T}$he conversations and correspondence with Paul made me do a lot of reflecting. As I thought about what had so dramatically shaped his life, making him into the man I knew and respected, I realized that it was time for me to reflect on my own life and where I was headed.

I had been blessed in being raised in a happy, secure home environment. I was the third in a family of six children, and our parents also cared for a foster brother, Gordon. "Three sons and three daughters," my father loved to say proudly.

"You were named after Princess Margaret Rose," he often reminded me. "Margaret Rose Fishback, that's what we decided to call you." My mother's background was Scottish; my father's parents had immigrated to Canada from Dusseldorf, Germany, before he was born. "There's a town on the border of Austria and Germany called Fishback, named for our family."

He was proud of his German heritage. But my first recollections of anything "bad" happening came as a result of my German background.

It happened in the first grade. I had trouble with the teacher, not because I was slow, but because I was bored. "Speak English or else," the teacher threatened. I must have picked up some German pronunciation from my father, for every time I pronounced words like free, tree, three, and other words like that, she would hit me on the knuckles with her pointer— a solid wooden stick with a black rubber tip. My knuckles were always red! I can still hear her say, "Don't speak with that German sound!" and down would come the pointer. Her "or else" threats embarrassed and scared me.

One day my father and I were sitting out on a log having one of our heart-to-heart talks, and I told him about it. "Be proud of your ancestry," he said, adding, "just remember what the Bible teaches, and the Ten Commandments, and don't talk back to your teacher."

It was my first encounter with animosity. Now, reflecting on that, I realized her hostility really had little or nothing to do with who I was. It was World War II. Later, in another class, when I wanted to do a research paper on my German background, my mother said "NO!" very firmly. Touchy-touchy, I thought, and never brought it up again, remembering my red knuckles and the first-grade teacher.

Another incident stands out when I felt the sting of a teacher's punishment. That time was in kindergarten. The teacher had a red leather strap that she used to swat us across our hands. She had gone out of the classroom and, kids being kids, we seized the opportunity—all of us, as I recall—to get up out of our desks and start swinging on them in the aisles. When the teacher returned and caught us, she lined us up and had us file into the cloakroom one by one. I could hear her hit the kids in front of me and suddenly tears started rolling down my cheeks. I felt so bad for my classmates, worse for them than I did for myself. But when it was my turn it hurt hardly at all. It was just a good sting. I was puzzled about that.

Didn't the teacher hit me as hard, because I was so tiny and fragile-looking? Did she think I was probably a follower and quite innocent? I reflected on that too as I called up memories from the past. I had cried for my classmates; I hadn't cried for myself. Crying for others is still something I do very easily; feeling Paul's pain made me weep. Crying is therapeutic. God values our tears; Psalm 56 says that He even records them. In many places we are told that God sees our tears, but we are promised that one day He will wipe away all tears from our eyes (Isaiah 25:8), and that there will be no more death or mourning or crying or pain (Revelations 21:4).

I kept my guardian angel busy, I'm quite certain. There was the day, when I was a small child, that my life was spared. My sister and I had been to Goodlett's Grocery Store and on the way home a cousin started chasing me. I darted into the street, into the path of an oncoming truck, and I was hit. The impact threw me onto the grass at our North Broadway Baptist Church.

The driver stopped, picked me up, and carried me to our home just a short block away. My sister was screaming and so was I—not because I was badly hurt, but more because I didn't want to be carried. And probably because I feared the reprimand which would be forthcoming from my parents, who always cautioned us to look both ways before crossing the street.

There was another time, when I was about thirteen, when a big bumblebee landed on me while I was hoeing potatoes in the garden. I was very nervous about bees, since we had lost an uncle to a bee sting. I started screaming and my brother Jim ran to rescue me. "No, no, don't touch me," I shouted, as my screams faded away, because suddenly I knew God was going to take care of me. It was like an instantaneous vision of the Lord coming down to help.

Childlike, I prayed, "Lord, take the bee away from me and I'll let You come into my life and direct me."

You aren't supposed to bargain with God! I can almost hear someone say that. But God knew I'd been giving Him a lot of thought, and this was my moment of reckoning! My older sister, you see, had become a Christian, and she kept urging me to ask Jesus into my life. I knew she prayed for me (I could hear her). I'd tell my mom and my sister, "I'm not interested. I want to become a concert pianist and an actress and a teacher. . . ." "She's a stubborn little thing," my mother declared more than once during those years.

I just didn't want anything to interfere with my childhood aspirations. And I certainly didn't want to change my ways or give up these dreams. What I didn't understand was that God doesn't take away, He only gives and enhances what He has already given. God is a giver. The best.

That day, after the bumblebee flew away without leaving behind its stinger, I threw down the hoe and told my mother I was going to be baptized at the church. I knew from that moment on that I would always want to show that Christ was in my life.

One other incident stood out as I reflected on my past, seeking to attach meaning to memories. I had observed how Paul's past had served as a wise teacher. He always would say, "Memories and mistakes should be guideposts, not hitching posts." I admired his concern for young people and could better understand why he had spent so many years working with Youth for Christ. I sensed a deep compassion in him for the less fortunate. And, above all, I knew that his first love was the Lord and it would always be that way. I had a love for children, too. But was there something else in my past that had stirred a desire in me to work with them?

And then I remembered. In school, teachers often asked me to help them work with other students. I had a natural knack for relating to children, but two girls seemed always to resent and even hate me. In all honesty, I can say that I grew up with two very mean girls as classmates. Regardless of what I did, they had it in for me. Maybe it was because one of these girls was very overweight, whereas I was always petite; today I'm still only 4' 10" in height.

One of the boys who lived near them became a sort of guardian for me through the years. Often he would jump between them and me and tell them to leave me alone. But one day he wasn't around to protect me, and neither was anyone else. The overweight girl got me where no one could see me and pushed me to the ground. Then she sat on me and tickled me until I was choking and could hardly breathe, and I thought I would die. If someone hadn't discovered what was happening, I might have suffocated. As it was, I ran home and collapsed. I was a very sick and frightened child, unable to attend school for many days. The teacher came to the house and apologized to me and my parents, and the girls were severely reprimanded and warned never to come near me again.

But I felt sadness in my heart for a long time. I wondered what it was that made them so hateful. I would have liked to help them; I would have been a good friend to them. Now, as I reflected on all this, I came to understand that God had put a love in my heart for those who needed to know about Him. There was a call upon my life and I would be true to it. I remember my father saying to me after this troublesome time, "What is God saying to you, Midge? What is God doing in your life?"

Always conscientious, I became even more so. My poetry of those days reflects where I was coming from and the direction I hoped to go. One such short poem reminds me even now of those learning days:

> People need your forgiveness
> Your words of encouragement sweet
> You'll find those people if you look—
> Perhaps they're 'neath your feet.

To this I added: Forgiveness is the fragrance the blossom leaves on the sole after it has crushed the flower.

I wanted to please the Lord, to live as one of His children.

Chapter Six

Beach Walk

In all their distress he too was distressed,
and the angel of his presence saved them.
In his love and mercy he redeemed them;
he lifted them up and carried them all the days of old.

Isaiah 63:9

*P*aul had been invited to speak at a youth retreat at a camp north of Kingston, over a hundred miles east of Toronto, on the Canadian Thanksgiving weekend. He'd called and asked if I would accompany him and play the piano for the meetings. Happily I'd accepted.

I was teaching school in Ingersoll, and after work on Friday afternoon I drove to my sister's apartment in a suburb just west of Toronto, right on Lake Ontario, where we had agreed to rendezvous. We arrived at about the same time.

I wasn't prepared for what happened shortly thereafter. I was in the bedroom adding some things to my suitcase when Paul walked in, hugged and kissed me, and then surprised me. "I love you and I know you love me. I have something for you."

Out came that little box every girl dreams of someday seeing in the hands of the man she loves. He opened it and there, nestled in velvet, was a sparkling diamond. Reaching for my hand, he said, "Can I put it on your finger?"

Shock registered on my face. Paul says at first it was sheer delight, but it quickly turned to almost sheer terror, and I started to cry. "My parents don't know!" I was an old-fashioned young woman in many respects, and accustomed to having things done in a very traditional way. I knew my parents loved Paul, but were they ready to welcome him into the family as a future son-in-law? If they knew all of Paul's background, would they really approve? Besides, we hadn't gone together very long. It was all so sudden!

Paul was trying to console and convince me at the same time. "Margie, it will all work out. Your parents like me. Your dad and I hit it off so well."

As it turned out, the ring was a size six, much too large for my size-four finger. Paul slipped it on and then we stood there laughing at the way it flopped around. "I'll speak to your parents and get your father's consent when we get back." He cupped my chin in his hands. "Does that make you feel better?"

I nestled against him. He was like a big, cuddly teddybear. "Paul, you know I love you. But yes, I want you to ask my dad for my hand. I guess I'm hopelessly sentimental. . . ."

I put the ring back in the box and slipped it into my purse. Then we were on our way to Echo Lake Conference Grounds, near Kingston. As we drove along, I kept taking the ring out and looking at and admiring it, and putting it back in my purse, and I went on doing this—putting it on and off—for many miles. En route, we discussed some of the obstacles that might confront us in the days ahead. How would we handle them? Neither of us came from an affluent family, and our jobs and our paychecks were all we had to survive on. Like most young people, we usually had more month left than money.

It was a gorgeous time of year. The autumn leaves had been falling from the maple trees, which were dressed in their finest yellow and orange, and the sumacs were the brightest red I'd ever seen. We marveled at the beautiful foliage, and I told Paul that fall was my favorite season.

We were to meet several carloads of people at Kingston for dinner before caravaning north to Echo Lake, some twenty miles farther. We were early. As we drove along, on impulse I said, "Let's go for a walk on the beach." We had been watching the yachts passing back and forth, making waves, and the beach looked inviting. Paul parked the car and we jumped out, leaving behind our shoes, and went off, barefoot, squishing the warm sand between our toes as we ran along.

We laughed at the gulls swooping down, scooping up fish in their sharp beaks. They were so graceful, soaring through the air, and I remember thinking "free as a bird."

The setting sun dancing on the water made it sparkle. It was incredibly beautiful. As we strolled along, arms around each other's waists, we picked up on our conversation. "How do you think I should approach your father?" Paul asked, and we bounced suggestions off each other.

"We've had so many weddings in our family recently," I pointed out. "Both my sister and my brother. I'm not so certain my parents are going to be ready for the idea of another wedding, even if it is next summer."

"How would you feel about the end of June or early July?" Paul asked.

As we talked, we'd grab each other's hands and dash in and out of the water as the waves rolled up on shore, leaving bubbles at our feet. Finally Paul looked at his watch and said it was time to turn back.

We laughed and made light talk some more, retracing our steps, and then picked up our discussion again, and it took a sudden serious turn. As the waves washed up over our footprints, they had left only one set of prints visible on our return journey to the car. Observing this, I said, "Maybe that's what will happen to us—maybe we'll be all washed up. Maybe our dreams are all going to wash away."

"No," Paul protested, "this makes me think of our future. On our wedding day, we two will become one, and oh, the joy that will be mine to go with you throughout our life together. See our footprints just up ahead? They're still there. Where they got washed out is just the troubled waters we're going to face. Every marriage faces that."

I was still apprehensive. "Will we have what it takes to weather the troubled waters?"

Paul stopped, looked deep into my eyes, and promised me, "We'll have it. If we love each other enough to fight for what we have, we'll make it. I've gone through enough, Margie, to know what fighting is all about. What we have is worth fighting for."

"What will happen when trouble comes that we just can't handle?" I stopped walking, and pointed even as I was asking the question. "Look, Paul, now there's only one set of footprints."

Paul sighed and was silent for a moment. His grip on my hand tightened reassuringly, and he said, "Margie, when the most troublesome times come, that neither one of us can handle, that's when the Lord will carry us both, as long as we maintain our faith and trust in Him."

It was such a beautiful thought, expressed with the utmost sincerity, that it momentarily took my breath away. "Ohhh," I remember saying, "that's wonderful." The poet in me stirred. How could I let this man go? Yet love demanded so much. Could I risk loving him with all my heart?

Then he playfully picked me up, swinging me into the air and saying, "See, like this."

I squealed and cried out, "I can't see you, I can't see you!" We were young and in love, serious and contemplative, but it was to be a happy outing and Paul felt the need to hear me laugh and make me smile. He knew that things had been difficult for me since I'd been hit by the bolt of lightning, that I still wasn't completely well and was on medication. I needed this weekend retreat as much as any of the students who would be attending. As he twirled me around in the air, I squealed some more.

"I'm here," he laughed, "I'm holding you, you're safe."

It all happened in the space of just a few minutes, but the impression it made lasted and will last forever. I remember how Paul gently put me down, how he kissed me tenderly. I remember how we continued walking on, arms around each other's waists. But as we walked, we continued to silently observe our two sets of footprints—and sometimes only one. And it set my mind to musing. I was quite absorbed in my thinking, almost to the point of abstraction.

We returned to the Holiday Inn where we were to meet the others. As we sat in the restaurant, waiting for them to arrive, I took a paper napkin and began jotting down some ideas and phrases.

"What are you doing?" Paul asked, as if he didn't already know. He'd become quite accustomed to my reaching for something to write on whenever we were together. Poems were always forming in my head, it seemed.

"Oh, just another poem." I smiled at him. "About our footprints in the sand."

He reached across the table, patting my hand. He loved my poetry and was always expressing surprise and appreciation. He was a great encourager.

Following dinner, we all piled back into our cars and drove on to Echo Lake. We found our cabins, unpacked our belongings, said our goodnights, and settled in for the evening. The girls in our cabin were giggling and having fun, and I found it difficult to join in. I was glad when they settled down and one by one fell asleep. But sleep eluded me.

I thought about the diamond in the box. I wondered if our relationship had proceeded too fast. We'd known each other only six weeks. What would my family say? My mind replayed our beach-walk conversation. And then I reached for my notepad, pen, and flashlight. The words that had been forming in my head since that afternoon began taking shape on the paper.

As if in a dream, I saw a story unfolding in my mind's eye. I saw myself walking along a beach with the Lord, our feet leaving footprints in the sand. Across the sky flashed scenes from my life, and for each scene I noticed two sets of footprints in the sand—my own, and those of the Lord. When the last scene of my life shot before me, I looked back and saw that there was only one set of footprints. I realized that this was at the lowest and saddest times of my life. I asked the Lord where He had been when I needed Him most.

The words tumbled out, easily, effortlessly.

> Lord, you told me when I decided to follow You,
> You would walk and talk with me all the way.
> But I'm aware that during the most troublesome times
> of my life there is only one set of footprints.
> I just don't understand why, when I needed You most,
> You leave me.

Then I wrote His reply.

He whispered, "My precious child,
I love you and will never leave you,
never, ever, during your trials and testings.
When you saw only one set of footprints
it was then that I carried you.

Suddenly I was aware that I was writing free verse, which was not at all usual for me. I was accustomed to writing in rhyming verse or couplets.

I looked at my watch. It was three a.m. I shivered, feeling the cool early-morning air. "You'd better get some shut-eye," I told myself, "or you won't be worth anything the rest of the day." Just before falling asleep I thought, "Now I've written this and I don't even have a title." Then I wondered, "Has this just been a dream?"

In the morning, upon awakening, I reached for the notepad, read the poem, and immediately the thought came: "Call it 'I Had a Dream.'"

And that's how I wrote the poem that the nurse read to my husband in his hospital bed so many years later. It came to be known by the title "Footprints," but to us it will always be a reminder of our beach walk. To us it symbolizes the time when we realized that God was saying that this would be a God-blessed marriage, and that He would always be there walking with us, carrying us when we needed to be carried—as, of course, He wants to do for all His children.

Chapter Seven

"I Had a Dream"

... God has said, "Never will I leave you;
never will I forsake you."

Hebrews 13:5

The weather was perfect that memorable fall weekend. Chipmunks ran freely around the grounds searching for food, and squirrels were filling their cheeks with nuts and hiding them in trees in preparation for the soon-coming winter. We enjoyed watching them. The sun shone, and the leaves glowed, and the whole scene was breathtakingly beautiful.

The next morning, according to our prearranged plan, I was the pianist for the retreat meetings. Paul delivered a message entitled "I Cannot Pray the Lord's Prayer." About a hundred young people from all over Ontario were there—teenagers from high schools, along with college and career young people. Paul explained what had happened when he worked for Youth for Christ and "borrowed" money without telling anyone, and how he had found himself unable to pray—God seemed distant. He spoke of how unworthy he had felt because he knew he'd failed God and those who trusted him.

I watched as the young people listened intently. "I couldn't say, 'Our Father which art in heaven,'" he said. Then he told them about his own father—the abuse he'd suffered, and how he finally had learned to love him after hating him and wanting to kill him for so many years. It was obvious to me that God was using the worst thing that had happened in Paul's life to show these young people God's mercy and loving Fatherliness.

I showed Paul the poem "I Had a Dream" that afternoon. "Paul, God has quieted my heart. My father isn't going to reject you when you ask him if you can marry me. That experience yesterday on the beach, and then writing this, has given me courage. God really did something very special for us yesterday—a beautiful visual lesson. God's promise to always be with us is the only possible way our marriage will work."

As Paul read the poem, he understood what I was talking about, and he asked if he could read it at the evening retreat service. His message to the young people was that God is always there for us, that, though unseen, He is with us to care for us and carry us through. The words he spoke made an impact. The audience sat spellbound. "When Margie and I walked along the beach, discussing our coming marriage, at one point I swooped her up and held her up high," he told the young listeners. "She laughed and protested, but she knew I had a hold on her, a firm grip that would not let go." Then he made it very personal for each of them. "It's the same with all of us. We can't see Jesus, but He guarantees in His Word that while we were yet sinners He died for us. That's His guarantee. You can't see Him, but He's there. . . believe that! There were many times when I seemed to be in utter darkness and I couldn't see Him. I was flailing and lashing out, and sometimes I didn't think He could still love me, but always He was there, carrying me. And that's what He will do for you too."

Then he read the poem. Later, several people told us you could have heard the proverbial pin drop as many young people made life-changing decisions about trusting Christ with their lives.

The next morning many asked for copies of the poem. I also gave a copy to Lloyd Smith ("Smitty"), Paul's buddy, an outstanding musician, who was going to compose a musical score for it as a wedding gift to us. Lloyd died shortly after that—he was fatally injured in an inner-city accident during his missionary work—so he was never able to complete the musical score. It was one of those times that we knew, in later reflection, that the Lord truly carried Paul, for Smitty's death was a great personal loss.

The next morning, following that glorious retreat weekend, everyone said their goodbyes and went in different directions. We stopped in Frankford for lunch and Paul introduced me to Mom and Dad Adams, his "foster" parents—the elderly couple he had been boarding with when he found Christ. Before leaving, they had a prayer with us about our new life together.

We laughed, sang, and joked all the way home. When we became weary, we turned up the radio volume to the highest level and opened the windows. Just before reaching the farm, Paul pulled to the side of the road and we had a time of prayer together. We were both quietly serious, wondering how my dad would react to what Paul was going to ask him. After all, Paul and I had really only had two dates. Even in my own mind the questions kept going around: *Do we truly know each other? I learned more about Paul this weekend than I've known before—we're so different—can it work?* Our backgrounds were exactly the opposite in every possible way.

A crackling fire greeted us, with Mom and Dad anxious to hear all about the retreat. Then I whispered to my mother that I needed to talk to her alone, and Paul was left standing in the kitchen, staring nervously at my father. He describes that encounter like this: "Margie's father was a big rough-hewn German farmer who was sitting there with his thumbs hooked in the bib of his overalls, looking me up and down as if I were a steer he might be considering for purchase."

My father had a wonderful sense of humor, and I think he knew all along what was coming, but he kept Paul in the hotseat for just a few moments. "You want to talk to me?"

"Yes sir."

"Well, did you have an accident?"

"No," Paul responded.

"Then what do you want to talk about?"

"Margie."

"What's wrong with Midge?" Dad asked.

"Nothing's wrong with her."

"Then what are you talking about?"

"I think I'm supposed to say, 'I would like to have your daughter's hand in marriage.'"

Paul said there was an awkward silence for what seemed like an eternity to him, but finally Dad said, "Well, what's wrong with the rest of her?" and he was grinning from ear to ear.

"All right, I'd like all of her," and Paul joined in grinning.

My father wanted to know if Paul really loved me, and told him he'd *better know*. "She's my little girl and I've taken good care of her all these years. Will you do the same? You must love her in good and bad times, and love her even more than you love yourself."

Paul gave a wonderful response to the earlier grilling and to my father's sentimental statements at the end: "Mr. Fishback, I will love Margie and I will honor her. I will try to make her life happy. But I'm not stupid. There are times when she's going to be unhappy. And when she's hurt, I will be there to comfort her. I don't want to take her away from your family, but I want her to be my wife. I want to belong to your family!"

The next thing Paul knew, my dad got to his feet, put his big callused hands on Paul's shoulders, and gave him a bone-crushing hug. "C'm'ere, son. . . let me welcome you to the family!"

And that's how my mother and I found the two of them. There was a lot of hugging going on in that old-fashioned kitchen that night. Then we all sat down and I shared with them the poem and our experience as we'd walked along the beach. My parents were deeply touched and immediately saw the significance of what had taken place.

I told them about waking up in the early hours of the morning and about how it seemed that God was in control of my hand and the pen as I wrote. "God impressed upon my heart two verses from the Bible," I said. "Here, let me read them for you." And I read Isaiah 63:9 and Hebrews 13:5.

The Isaiah passage says, "In all their distress he too was distressed, and the angel of his presence saved them. In his love and mercy he redeemed them; he lifted them up and carried them all the days of old."

And Hebrews 13:5 states, "Keep your lives free from the love of money and be content with what you have, because God has said, 'Never will I leave you; never will I forsake you.'"

Father gave us his blessing, and we made our wedding plans in the months that followed. We were able to see each other on only two special occasions before our wedding date of July 10, 1965.

Chapter Eight

"A New Life"

"It's a new life, oh, how He changed me,
A new life, He rearranged me,
A new life, richer and fuller,
A wonderful, wonderful life. . . ."

I also wrote a new song that weekend at the retreat,
which was introduced there. The words speak of the
new life in Christ—deeper and wider, greater and
more wonderful than the old life; little did Paul and I
know the full meaning those words would have in our
lives as man and wife. Time after time we would be
made to realize how fragile life is and how dependent
man is on God.

We had a great honeymoon week, going to Kingston
and retracing our "footsteps" walk, this time sharing
the confidence that our step of commitment had given
both of us.

Then it was back to Toronto. Paul was still manag-
ing film rentals at the Christian bookstore, and I
began teaching in a school in the Yorkville district, at
that time a rather tough neighborhood in the heart
of Toronto. Weekends found us doing presentations

for youth groups. Paul's "Gospel Magic with a Message," a magician show tied in to biblical messages, was a big attraction. We were kept very busy.

From almost the first day we were married, Paul had serious health problems. He had had rheumatic fever as a child, after his mother died, and had spent about a year in a brace. The disease had left him with a weakened heart. Sometimes I found it hard to be patient with his weakness.

In November, after four months of marriage, I called my mother with another complaint: "Every time I cook something, Paul ends up getting sick. Here I am going to a gourmet cooking class, and he gets sick."

"What are you putting in your cooking?" my mother asked.

"Lots of spices," I told her.

"Why are you using all those spices?" she asked.

"Mom, I got this beautiful, gigantic spice-rack set for a wedding gift. I have to use those spices. They're wonderful!"

"They aren't so wonderful if they make your husband sick. You've got to make a decision—either you cook your own meals using your spices and cook Paul's meals separately, or you cook in order for Paul to survive and be well so the two of you can enjoy your married life. My dear, you've got to make up your mind—for better or for worse!" And down went the receiver.

Everything seemed to be working against me. To me, cooking was one of the central things about being married. Good cooking, fellowship—these were important to a marriage. I tried baking—no success. Failure after failure. I despaired. Finally, with every cake turning out like Jell-O, Paul got around to looking at the oven and, of course, it wasn't working properly. I couldn't help blaming him for all those ruined desserts—why hadn't he guessed that the oven was the problem?

At one point Paul was so sick with a serious ear infection that he became delirious and my brother Jim ended up taking care of him while I worked. When I came home, I found a note saying he'd been taken to the hospital. I had to get compassionate in a hurry. I got ready to go to the hospital, but just then my brother brought Paul home and I could see he really had a high fever. "You must get up in the middle of the night and look after him," Jim instructed me. "See to it that he gets his pills when he needs to take them."

I dutifully gave Paul his medicine, had him drink lots of water, and held his hand. In the morning my brother came over and said, "Now, Margie, I want to show you how to change his dressing."

I protested. I knew what a mess his ear was, and I was squeamish. "Look, he's your husband," Jimmy said. I learned to change the dressing, but I wasn't happy about it!

We didn't go home for Christmas that first year of our marriage. I knew I had to get a handle on my emotions, and I realized shamefully that I had been a failure in our marriage thus far. I was a very fussy house-fanatic—thinking I had to keep our apartment just so. Nurturing our relationship was taking second place to the adjustments of marriage. Thankfully, I came to my senses and began to focus on my husband and the ministry God had entrusted to us.

We got into children's ministry quite by accident—at least, that's the way it seemed to us, but we know, of course, that nothing is happenstance with God. Paul had been invited to speak at a church for a week of evening meetings in Timmins, a city over four hundred miles due north of Toronto. When he walked into the church on the first night, he was shocked to see it full of *little kids*. He was accustomed to speaking to teenagers. Then he found out what had happened—a flyer advertising his coming had a misprint. Instead of inviting youth "15 to 21," the flyer said "5 to 12"!

As it turned out, it was a wonderful week, with Paul doing illusions, rope and handkerchief tricks, "phantom box" tricks, a "Bible Tear" trick, and other object lessons, all demonstrating biblical truths in memorable ways. I hadn't gone along to Timmins, but I was aware of what had happened because Paul phoned me right after the first meeting. That had sent me to my knees, and I'd enlisted the help of two other teachers as well. When Paul returned home and told me what had taken place with the children, I wasn't surprised. *God does answer prayer.* "Paul, you'd make a great children's worker," I told him.

At first he objected, but then he began to see that God had given him a heart for children. He realized in the months that followed, as he became more and more involved with children, that God had been putting him in touch with an entire generation that was desperately trying to find alternatives to isolation. Many of these were latchkey kids—with working moms and dads, if they were even lucky enough to have both—and they knew about loneliness.

Together Paul and I confronted what was becoming very obvious to us—together we made a team, because my interest as a teacher was with younger children.

Nine months later, we knew it was time for Paul to leave the bookstore and step out on his own in the film-rental business. We became the new Toronto representatives, not only of Gospel Films, but of most of the other major studios producing Christian films at that time. Paul also began doing more traveling, working with the well-known country-and-western singer and Hollywood personality Redd Harper.

I was trying to hold down a full-time teaching position, and travel with Paul when possible. We were entertaining children all over the country. In particular, Paul was being asked to appear in purely secular magic shows during the winter months—January through March—at some of the biggest amusement parks in the U.S., including Six Flags Magic Mountain in Atlanta, Busch Gardens in Florida, Knott's Berry Farm, the Japanese Gardens, and the Crocodile Farm, all in the Los Angeles area, Disneyland in southern California, and Disneyworld in Florida.

In the summer, when I was on vacation from teaching and the film business was slow, we concentrated on ministry in churches, camps, and Daily Vacation Bible Schools in and around Toronto.

This routine took its toll, however, and I knew I had to make a choice. Would I continue to hold down a full-time teaching position, or should I resign and travel with Paul?

Chapter Nine

"Letter from a Friend"

"I am writing to say how much I care
for you and how much I want you
to know me better. . . ."

$\mathscr{F}$aced with the choice of whether to continue teaching, or to travel with my husband, I chose the latter. It was on one of our trips, in July 1966, that God got my attention in a most dramatic way. It happened on a Pennsylvania turnpike in the States.

We were returning from vacationing and the National Audio Visual Convention, and found ourselves caught in a tornado. Animals were being blown away, and we watched, horror-stricken, as a van we'd been following, loaded with nuns, was blown right off the hill. There was no way we could stop, and although we later reported the accident, we never heard what happened to the nuns. It was all Paul could do to keep the car on the road. We finally found protection under an overpass.

The next day, still very shaken by the experience and our near brush with death, I sat down, pen in hand, and these words came out on paper:

Letter from a Friend

I am writing to say how much I care
for you and how much I want you
to know me better.
When you awoke this morning, I exploded
a brilliant sunrise through your window
trying to get your attention. You rushed off.
Later, I spotted you walking and talking
with some friends. I bathed you in
warm sunshine. I perfumed the air
with nature's sweet scent. You rushed off.
You didn't notice me.
Then I shouted to you in a tornado.
I painted you a beautiful rainbow
in the sky. Then you gave me a glance.
Still you rushed off.
That evening I spilled moonbeams
in your face. I sent a cool breeze
to rest you and take away your fear.
I watched over you as you slept. I shared
your thoughts. You were faintly aware
I was so near. I've chosen you. I have
a special task for you. I hope you will
talk to me soon. Only I brought you through
the storm. Others saw no morn.
I remain near. I am your friend.
I love you very much.

Your Friend, Jesus

I read the poem to Paul and we discussed its meaning. Our lives were on a fast track and we knew it.
Did we need to slow down? Did we need to stop, to

think about where we were headed? Did we need to get off altogether?

We didn't change our ways for a while. At first the "winter vacations" to the U.S. and the long-distance traveling were enjoyable, and I liked the fast-paced routine. I traveled with Paul throughout the winter and spring of 1968, right up to the time we had a little one of our own.

Christina (Tina) was born on Victoria Day, 1968. I wasn't well, and my mother came and stayed with us. It seemed that I had built up some kind of an immunity to pain and had a violent reaction to medication—like an epileptic seizure—when Tina was born. My heart actually stopped. It was felt that I had suffered from spinal meningitis after being struck by lightning five years earlier, and the doctors warned me that I could expect to have some health problems from this about every seven years. I was warned against becoming overly fatigued, or being under too much stress.

We had a beautiful baby, however, and once I was back on my feet, this new little life drew out the mothering instincts in me, and Paul became a wonderful father. The following summer, I once again joined Paul in his travels, this time with a baby in tow.

It was in 1970 that I finally really began to admit that our lives were headed in the wrong direction. Paul was making good money performing at the secular jobs, but we weren't getting ahead financially. I could see that our film business was suffering as we left it in the hands of college students; we just weren't "minding the store" at home enough. I was also concerned that Paul had become somewhat cynical about Christian ministry. In some respects, he was justified—churches often didn't pay on time, nor did they begin to match what he could receive in the secular world. His bitterness about the way churches sometimes treated outside speakers such as ourselves began to show.

Our second daughter, Paula, was born in January 1971. Another new life.

The years were going by so fast, and it seemed that our own lives were unraveling at the same speed. With two little ones to care for, I found myself staying home and resenting it when I did have to join Paul in some city, usually in the U.S. We had a beautiful home in Don Mills, one of the nicer neighborhoods in the northern part of Toronto. We had a swimming pool, a couple of late-model cars, and credit cards that we used often. But we didn't have a normal family life.

The tension between Paul and me increased. We seemed to be slipping farther and farther apart.

It was on a return trip from Warsaw, Indiana, where we had been at a Ken Anderson Film Conference, that Paula—then about three—got my attention. We were walking through an airport when she sat down right in the middle of nowhere and couldn't go on. She was one sick little girl. She had contracted scarlet fever. Paul hoisted her on his shoulders and we walked on. I had an instant flashback to the beach walk and the footprints in the sand, and knew that

God was still carrying us along, but it was time to get back in step with Him.

It was as if I heard God say, "You keep rushing off. . . I hope you will talk to me soon."

Chapter Ten

Trials and Testings

"... during your trials and testings,
when you saw only one set of footprints
it was then that I carried you."

The decision was made. No more traipsing around the U.S. doing magic acts in secular settings for the Powers family. I had been praying for a long time that we would get out of the Hollywood kind of life we'd been in for too many years. A verbal battle, waged on a Los Angeles freeway while we were trying to maneuver our way through Friday-night traffic, precipitated this decision.

We'd been invited to meet friends for dinner, but something inside me exploded en route. "I'm leaving you and taking the girls with me!" Paul was stunned, but so was I at this unexpected outburst. Somehow we got through the dinner hour, and on the way back to Redd Harper's home, where we were staying, we were able to talk out our situation. We loved each other, we had precious children, we were God's children, and we had a great ministry. "All of that should come first, Paul," I gently reminded him. That night, we prayed and entrusted ourselves and the future to God. We also asked our good friend Redd to pray for us and the direction our lives should go.

Upon our return to Toronto, we were confronted with an enormous stack of bills. "Please handle it, Margie," Paul said. "You know I'm not good at it." Yes, I did know, but what a struggle it proved to be. Together we plunged into our summer ministry work, but it was a troublesome time—a time of trial and testing the likes of which we'd never experienced before.

The franchise film business was experiencing a major slump and we were urged to sell the business. Still we hung on, hoping for a holiday upswing, but as we headed into fall and the holiday season it didn't materialize. Christmas 1972 looked bleak.

Hitting rock bottom was something neither of us had anticipated when we told God we'd put Him first and give up the other lifestyle. Poverty? I couldn't believe it.

I urged Paul to go out and try to collect some of the money that eight churches in the Toronto area owed us for fall children's crusades. None had paid him at the time he spoke. It proved to be the most humiliating day of his life, netting not quite forty dollars.

Discouraged, Paul handed the money to me upon his return so I could go out and get groceries. "Spend it carefully, Margie," he cautioned, "it's all we've got. I've put gas in the car for the trip to the farm." We were planning to drive to my parents' farm the next morning to spend Christmas day with the family.

The girls were bundled up and we left to go shopping. Two hours later we returned. I felt good about some bargains I'd found, but Paul was angry, especially when Tina showed him a roll of gold wrapping paper.

His frustration boiled up and spewed out as he screamed at me for being so wasteful. The atmosphere at dinner was depressing and we picked at our food. Little Tina's tearful blue eyes mirrored the pain we were all feeling.

Paul and I went to his downstairs office to do some gift-wrapping. Tina was trying to help. At one point Paul sarcastically said, "Tina, would you go upstairs and get that gold paper your mother wasted the money on?"

If I hadn't felt cut down to size before, I certainly did then. Tina took her time about coming back, so Paul stormed up the stairs. I was on his heels. There sat Tina, in an alcove just off the living room, surrounded by wads of gold paper and three pairs of scissors. Gobs of sticky-tape were all over her as well as the rug. And the single sheet of gold paper? She'd used it all trying to wrap something that looked like a shoebox.

Anger flooded Paul's face as he raced across the room, grabbed her by one arm, and jerked her into the air, slapping her hard several times. Tina's screams and sobs made him realize what he was doing, and he stopped, letting go of her as she fell to the floor, a terrified, crying little girl.

I was in shock. Was this the Paul who claimed to love God and little children?

For Paul it was a flashback to his own childhood, when he had been so abused at the hands of his raging, drunken father. Later, he confessed that all he could think of for the rest of the evening was, *You're just like your father . . . you're a coward who beats little children . . . just like your father . . . you're no good, no good, no good. . . .*

I put Tina to bed, comforting her as best I could.

The next morning, as we prepared to go to the farm, Paul tripped and almost fell over the box Tina had wrapped in the gold paper. Still irritated, he kicked it out of the way, but at that moment Tina ran to the box, picked it up, and ran back to Paul. "Here, Daddy, it's for you," she whispered.

Paul took it and shook it gently, but it was very light and nothing rattled inside. The tape all over the box made it hard to unwrap and his frustration and impatience once again spilled over. He ripped it open, but when he looked inside, there was nothing there. With his temper no longer in check, he said sharply, "Christina! Don't you know you should put something in a box before you wrap it up as a gift?"

Tears were streaming down her little face as she said, "But Daddy, I *did* put something in it. I blew kisses into it! It's full of love just for you!"

An empty box, but strangely, wonderfully full! It was *the* gift Paul needed the most. Right there in the hallway, he dropped to his knees, hugged Tina, begged her forgiveness, and then hugged Paula and me, begging our forgiveness as well. His sobs were deep, coming from the depths of his being.

Paul received a healing within at that moment—the enemy, his anger, died. He cried out to God for help and received it.

But I had been wrong too. I'd been upset and nagging at him. "I helped cause all of this, Paul," I confessed, "but we love each other and I know God's going to help us."

We still have that golden box. A reminder of one of the *best* Christmases we've ever had. It had been a time of trial and testing, but God had carried us through.

Chapter Eleven

Wings

How priceless is your unfailing love!
Both high and low among men find refuge in the
shadow of your wings.

Psalm 36:7

*A*ngels! Our little girls knew about angels. For one thing, in the winter we loved lying down in the snow, spreading our arms, and making angels with wings. Of course, we told them about angels too, introducing them at a very young age to Bible stories that spoke of them as "ministering spirits" for God's people. But we came to know about angels one summer in a very real way.

When our daughter Paula was just beginning to talk, in her early twos, we headed for a crusade north of Peterborough in Ontario. A friend called shortly before we left and said, "Stop by on your way. We'll picnic in the back yard."

It was a fun time. We sat in a circle in our friends' beautiful yard, our backs to the house, enjoying the picnic. Our hostess' brother came driving up on his Harley-Davidson. Instead of putting it on its kickstand, he leaned it against the house.

Paula climbed down from my lap and, unknown to us, was playing around the motorcycle at the front wheel. It happened so fast. One moment she was laughing and running around, the next moment she was screaming as the motorcycle fell on top of her, crushing her with its weight.

Everyone jumped up and ran to her, the men lifting the motorcycle off her little body. It was obvious that she was in serious condition; one of the parts of the cycle had gone into her head, puncturing it with a deep wound. Paula was screaming as Paul picked her up and ran to the car. Blood was spurting everywhere. "Oh, dear God, help us and spare her!" I cried it out over and over again. Feeling panic-stricken but, amazingly, still in control, I cautioned Paul, "Keep holding your hand on her head. Press to stop the blood."

I got into the car and Paul handed Paula to me. Her little hands were fluttering and her whole body was in shock, shaking. I wiped the blood off one of her hands, put her little thumb in her mouth, and held it there, applying pressure against the roof of her mouth.

Someone immediately called the hospital, alerting them that we were on the way. Quickly the hospital called for policemen; some met us, sirens blaring, while others cleared the highway. The emergency team was waiting and ready at the hospital. She was rushed inside.

As they examined her, the doctors asked us to step close. "Look down here, Mrs. Powers," one of them said, and I looked. It was like looking into a deep well.

"That's where the damage is. Amazing that she's alive!" I was fully aware that it was only because of God.

Had the wound been more than a few hairs closer, it would have punctured the brain. It required thirteen stitches, but we were able to take her home from the hospital later that evening. Both Paul and I were in absolute awe as we experienced the presence and strength of the Lord.

I put Paula in her crib and positioned myself in a chair alongside. I stayed awake, praying, thanking God for sparing the life of our precious little one. At one point I felt a coolness on my face and moved back. Still I felt the gentle breeze. Paula whimpered just a little, opened her eyes as I bent over her, and said, "Wings, Mommy, wings."

Wings, Mommy, wings. I sat down and repeated Paula's words. She sighed a little sigh, and once again I heard her say, "Wings . . . wings."

"Oh, thank You, thank You Lord, for what You have done!"

I breathed another prayer of gratitude for God's watchcare. A little later I went into our bedroom, awakened Paul, and told him "Paula's guardian angels are watching over her." Then I told him what had happened.

"Let me sit with her now," he said. "You need some rest. She's going to be all right, but let me watch her now."

I agreed, lay down, and fell asleep peacefully. The last thing I remember is the gentle breeze and *"Wings, Mommy, wings."*

Chapter Twelve

"My Angels Will Help You"

For he will command his angels concerning you
To guard you in all your ways. . . .

Psalm 91:11

The motorcycle falling on little Paula was not to be our only encounter with her guardian angels. We are sure that years later, when she fell into the whirlpool of water and was swept over the falls in the summer of 1989, it was a true miracle that her life was spared. The odds of someone surviving a sixty-eight-foot fall like that are very slim. Paula too has a way of keeping her guardian angels busy.

On one occasion when our daughters were still little, friends met us at our home in Don Mills for dinner. We planned to go to the Prince Hotel for the occasion. We were all chatting in the front hall, waiting for Paul. He came bounding down the stairs, reached the landing, and tripped. Everyone heard the sound—like a yard-stick cracking—and just knew he'd broken his leg. Still he insisted on going out, and there was no way anyone could convince him otherwise. During the dinner hour, his leg swelled incredibly. Although he bravely tried to conceal it, there was no mistaking it: something was terribly wrong, and he was in excruciating pain. He leaned heavily on our friends, Ernie and Phyllis Hayes, as we made our way out of the restaurant.

"Paul, you must have that looked at," they insisted, and this time he didn't object. We decided to go directly to the hospital from the hotel. Our friends agreed to drive the girls home, and said they'd wait for our return.

Before parting, seven-year-old Paula said, "Daddy, I want to pray for your leg," and she laid her hands on his leg, closed her little eyes, and prayed: "God, please heal our daddy's leg because he doesn't have time to be sick." Then she looked up at Paul and very confidently said, "My angels will help you."

I drove the car to the hospital, and on the way I looked across at Paul. In spite of the pain, we couldn't help smiling at each other as we spoke of Paula's sweet and simple faith. But then he pulled his pantleg up, glanced down, and said, "Margie, from the kneecap to below the ankle it's *really* swollen."

It took eight minutes to get from the hotel to the hospital emergency entrance. I jumped out and came around to the other side of the car. "Please sit here, Paul," I said, "while I go in and get a wheelchair and an attendant. Can you lift your leg out?" I asked. "Careful . . . careful . . . ," I cautioned. I stooped down to assist him, and when we pulled his pantleg up again, the swelling was no longer there. A surprised look crossed his face, then he cautiously flexed the leg while I looked on in awed silence.

"Margie! The pain . . . it's gone. I can bend it! And look! The swelling is gone!"

We looked at each other in amazement. "God answered Paula's prayer," he said quietly. "Thank You, God, and thank you, angels."

Still I insisted he go in and have the leg X-rayed. The X-rays showed nothing, not so much as a small fracture. The doctor and nurses on duty were just as shocked as we were when we told them what had happened.

All the way home we kept shaking our heads. "I can't believe it," one or the other of us would say. It wasn't that we didn't have the faith to believe that God could instantaneously knit broken bones back together, but it was so overwhelming.

When we drove up to our home, our friends and Tina and Paula rushed out to the car. "Daddy, Daddy!" the girls shouted.

"Paul, you drove the car!" Phyllis said.

"Why are you back so soon?" Ernie asked.

"I know why," Paula said shyly, giving her daddy a big hug.

She could just as well have said, "I told you so!"

Chapter Thirteen

Out of the Mouths of Babes

From the lips of children . . . you have
ordained praise. . . .

Psalm 8:2

Through the years, in our travels, Paul read my
poetry on many, many occasions. Often the poems
were used in church bulletins. Paul's messages—
given throughout Ontario and to the farthest corner
by the Quebec border—were frequently taped.

During this time, I also wrote a lot of choruses, and
we taught them as we moved about. These were
catchy little songs that adults and children caught on
to easily. In particular, the audiences seemed to enjoy
singing "Do You Know?" (to the tune "Do, Re, Me")
and "Praise the Lord, I Know" (to the tune "It's a
Small, Small World").

In New York State, I taught the folk tune for "King
of Kings." In fact, Paul brought this back with him
from a trip he'd made to Israel, so I wrote the words
for "King of Kings, Lord of Lords." Also right at this
time, because Paul was starting to gain a little weight
and the girls and I were doing what we called our

"aerobic tunes," I made up a fun-tune which every-one enjoyed entitled "Ho, Ho, Ho, Hosanah!" It soon became a favorite. We made a trip to the west coast some months later and found people there already singing and teaching this catchy little chorus. "Paul, I'm happy and grateful that these choruses are moving across the country so quickly," I said.

Our girls were growing up and participating in meetings. We had given them ventriloquist dolls. Tina had named hers Cindy; Paula called hers Heather. This became their introduction into joining us in our ministry presentation. Not long after that, Paul him-self got a "vent doll," as they are called in the trade, who was named TJ (Timmy Jimmy). Later he acquired Rusty, who became his companion wherever he spoke until the day Rusty was stolen. Then, through God-orchestrated events, Andy came into Paul's possession, and became the indispensable door-opener to many places that would otherwise be unwilling to admit someone like Paul and his family. We became, in every sense of the word, a real family team.

It was during the mid-seventies, following a return trip from Israel, that Paul experienced a "stress attack" (called that by the doctors who attended him). He was ordered to cut back and take it easy. Our film business was in decline and when a Christ-ian bookstore in Toronto offered to buy it, the sale was consummated. It was the same bookstore where Paul had worked in the 1960s, and now he was hired back to manage the film-rental business on a salaried basis. I helped, doing part-time work as a bookkeeper.

For the next seven years we worked there, as well as continuing our ministry throughout Canada and parts of the upper United States.

"Cutting back" just didn't seem to be in our vocabulary, however—"Little People's" ministry presented so many needs and opportunities that we felt we couldn't ignore. We had an annual two-month leave of absence from the bookstore in July and August to do Daily Vacation Bible Schools in the area, and since the film business was slow then, the arrangement worked out nicely.

Overscheduling was common for us. Not that we meant to do it, but it happened. Once again God used one of our daughters to get our attention. It happened one summer at a church in Fergus, Ontario, where we were teaching. Tina, eight at the time, participated in the programs with us. Five-year-old Paula, however, stayed at our camping trailer with a baby-sitter. She was a happy and contented child.

Returning to the trailer to pick up a piece of forgotten equipment one noon, Paul stopped to say hi to Paula, who was playing in the shade of a tree with a crèche set he'd brought back from Israel for her. He looked down at the set and asked, "Honey, where are Mary and Joseph? I don't see them."

"Oh, it's okay, Daddy," Paula replied. "Mary and Joseph are off on a crusade, and the three wise men are baby-sitting Jesus."

It stopped Paul in his busy tracks. He did a double-take. When he returned to the car where I was waiting, he said, "You won't believe what just happened!" He looked somewhat shaken.

"Are you all right?" I asked, placing my hand on his arm.

"Yeah . . . yeah, I'm okay, but Margie, I have a feeling the Lord has just used our daughter to get our attention." And he told me about the passing conversation.

"When I left her, she added, 'It's okay, Dad. Mary and Joseph are just like you and Mama—they're always gone.'"

I repeated Paula's words: *Mary and Joseph are just like you and Mama—they're always gone.* Paul," I said, "that's cute, but it's not funny."

"I know," he replied, glancing sideways at me. His face wore a faraway expression. Once again I guessed that Paul was thinking of his own lonely childhood.

That night, as Paul and I picked up on that conversation again, he commented, "Margie, do you suppose God is telling us to 'be still and know that He is God'?"

We talked about that. One of the emphases in our meetings with parents was to urge them to have time with their kids. Now we had to face the facts—we were too busy ourselves, and it wasn't just for the sake of ministry. We were getting paid well for what we did, and we had worked out a method whereby churches were actually paying. In the process, however, the girls weren't getting as much as they needed from us.

"Time to practice what we preach," Paul said, and he was so right.

We began scheduling special "family nights" into our itinerary, when the girls could choose what they wanted to do. We held to it from that point on, and we hold to it even today. We made a promise to God, to each other, and to the children, that even though the ministry to children was demanding, it would never shove our own daughters from the center of our love and concern. We believe this is as God would have it; for He Himself established the family as a unit. Never again would our daughters be able to say we were always gone.

In my husband's book, *Too Tough to Cry*, in making reference to this incident in our lives, he wrote: "God forbid that families should wind up 'castaways' on the barren islands of busyness, or that their children should be abused or neglected. Unfortunately, it happens much too often."

As we came to the close of the 1970s, we wrestled with finding God's will concerning one of the most important decisions we'd ever faced. We felt, for many reasons, that it was time to uproot our family. But it would mean leaving so much behind. There was a tug-of-war going on in our hearts and minds. What were we supposed to do?

Chapter Fourteen

Moving Day

If the Lord delights in a man's way,
he makes his steps firm. . . .

Psalm 37:23

A new decade. A new life. It was July 1980, and it was moving day.

The moving van was being loaded with our furniture and belongings. Neighbors, family, and friends were sitting around the inside walls of our home, quietly visiting, each dreading the moment of farewell hugs and goodbyes. "We've got to run to the lawyer to sign and pick up some documents," Paul said. "Hang tight, everyone, don't go away, we'll be back shortly."

We jumped in our van and Paul pulled away speedily. Not only did we pick up boxes of material, but we signed the final papers for the sale of our home. Then we loaded the six cartons from the lawyer in the van, which was already practically bulging, and the argument began. "Paul, you know these boxes have got to go with us. They're much too important to load on the moving van."

"No way," he said firmly, without even glancing at me. "We have a twenty-five-hundred-mile drive ahead of us—it's a long way to Vancouver, Margie—we need stretching room in this van. You can't load it to the ceiling with boxes."

"Oh, but we must!" I countered. "Paul, the things in these boxes are absolutely irreplaceable. What if something happened . . . ," and my voice trailed off. Paul's face was resolute and he just drove on, shaking his head.

I had vacillated about moving anyway—one moment excited, the next not overly enthused about going off to British Columbia—and now this. We didn't need a disagreement at this stage—it was all so emotional anyway. One last try . . ."Paul, my poems are in one of those boxes—all of them, Paul, everything I've ever committed to paper, they're my collections—and certificates, the blueprints for your magic illusions, awards. . . ."

"Trust me, Margie," he said, firmly but kindly. "That moving van is loaded with things that are dear and valuable to us. Look, those moving companies are bonded, they have to be trusted. Come on now, lighten up," he added, reaching over to pat my face. A loving gesture, a sweet look on his face as he caught my eye, and I knew I needed to listen to him.

We bounded out of the van and carried the boxes, which were already sealed tightly, over to the moving van. "Just a few more boxes, guys," Paul said. "Looks like you've finished."

"Ready to go!" said the driver.

Paul and I did a quick walk through the house, making certain nothing had been overlooked. Our friends, neighbors, and family members were no longer sitting on the floor; now they all stood around in little clusters. It was time to say goodbye. All day I'd been fighting back the tears. More than once I'd had to beat a hasty retreat to the bathroom, close and lock the door, and dab at my eyes. Now they overflowed. It didn't help when I looked at the dear familiar faces. Others were crying too. Goodbyes are never easy. But we had lived in that house for thirteen years—we had made it a lovely home—and now we were leaving it and all these dear ones behind to go into uncharted territory.

As we pulled away that afternoon, with everyone waving, blowing kisses, and calling out final farewells, I had to take charge and remind myself why we were doing this.

The restless feelings had begun some months earlier. In fact, it had been in the fall of the previous year that we began to talk about these feelings to each other. "We've been going to the same churches and camps for almost fifteen years, year after year," Paul said. "Perhaps it's time for a change. Besides, the winters here in Ontario are long and cold. . . ."

I had to admit he was right. About twice a year—we could count on it—Paul would get walking pneumonia. "And remember all those housing tracts and new churches we saw being built in Vancouver when we were there a year ago? We keep talking about going into full-time ministry. If we're going to do it, we should do so before the girls get any older," I reminded Paul. "Tina will be in junior high soon and she'll have to switch schools anyway."

Back and forth the reasoning went. "Let's put the house up for sale and see what happens. It'll be a sign. Sort of like Gideon's fleece," I said.

But the house didn't sell on the market in September, and we shelved the idea of moving. Still, we kept praying, asking God to make his will for our lives very plain.

In conversation with friends at a conference for pastors, Paul learned that B.C. was considered the "new frontier" of ministry in Canada. Remembering the enthusiastic reception we'd received when we ministered there, Paul agreed. He came home and once again the subject came up. "B.C. is booming!" he exclaimed. "What potential for ministry, Margie!" His eyes sparkled.

Paul and his pastor friends had gotten together at this conference and prayed about this possible move for us and our desire to go into full-time ministry. I had been giving it a lot of thought and prayer too. I looked up into Paul's dear face and said, "Paul, the potential is there; all we need is the faith."

Once more the house went up for sale—this time in May. Another fleece—the same one that had failed seven months before—and by the end of June the house was sold. Such excitement at the Powers' household!

"How will we support ourselves, Paul?" I had worried even before the house went back on the market.

"You know it will take time to get a full-time ministry started."

Within moments Paul had that "problem" solved. Or would it be more accurate to say that, once again, God orchestrated the events of our lives in such a way that we knew his footprints preceded ours? A job offer from International Audio Visual and Faith Films, Ltd., a film rental and supply company in Vancouver, paved the way. Paul was hired to do the promotion work for the new Focus on the Family film series, featuring Dr. James Dobson. "And of course," he was told, "you'll be sales rep for all of the other products we handle." The timing was perfect.

These were my thoughts as our heavily loaded van pulled away. One last glance backward as we left the familiar street and neighborhood. "We're on our way, family," Paul cried out. "Altogether now," he said: *"Vancouver, here we come!"*

Chapter Fifteen

Missing! Gone! Lost!

"When things go wrong, as they sometimes will,
When the road you're trudging seems all up hill . . .
Stick to the fight when you're hardest hit,
It's when things seem worst that you must not quit."

Edgar A. Guest

*W*e were lounging around the pool at the world-renowned Banff Springs Hotel in beautiful Alberta. It was a much-needed treat we were giving ourselves before settling in to the work that awaited us in Vancouver. Tina's school chum was working at the hotel for the summer so we had an added excuse to spend the weekend there. We relaxed completely, the long trip from eastern Canada behind us.

"Let's go to Lake Louise," Paul said. We did, and there we met Cliff and Billie Barrows. Cliff was one of the Billy Graham Team members, and a dear Christian brother.

On the road again, I voiced my concern once more about the cartons we'd put on the moving van at the last minute. "You know everything's going to have to come off the van and go into storage for a month, Paul," I said. "I sure hope we don't lose anything."

"Margie, have you been fretting about that all across the country?"

"Well . . . yes, I'm afraid so," I responded. "'Oh, ye of little faith,' right?" I tried to sound upbeat.

Paul reached over and patted me. "It's not that you're lacking in faith, Margie; you're human, and your concerns are real. God understands about our humanness. But let's finish out this relaxation interlude by having a good time, okay?"

I nodded in agreement.

Soon the blissful, all-too-brief holiday was over. We arrived in Vancouver the first week of August and found a place to stay for the month, until we could move into a home we hoped to purchase on the first of September. However, that house was sold, and we were delayed in getting another home.

And then moving-in day arrived! Everything was accounted for, the movers claimed. I walked from room to room looking at the boxes. Noticing my concern, one of the men said, "It's all here, ma'am," as he wiped the perspiration from his brow. Paul signed the papers and they left.

Surrounded by cartons and furniture, we began unpacking, setting things in place. But where were the boxes we'd put on the van at the last moment?

"You'll run across them, Margie," Paul reassured me. "Just keep going."

And so I kept going.

So did Paul and the girls. Happy shouts from Tina and Paula let us know they were finding their favorite things.

"Oh . . . look at this lamp," I groaned, as I discovered one was broken. When it came to unpacking the china, there were more disappointments and groans. Moving carries with it a certain amount of risk, of course, and we were finding out what that was all about.

By the next day, when most of the boxes had been shifted to appropriate rooms and many had been unpacked, the six cartons from the lawyer's office had still not been found. We checked and double-checked. "Paul, they aren't here. They're missing. Let's face it, they're gone."

Then Paul began berating himself. "Margie, I'm so sorry. I should have listened to you. Just as soon as the phone is connected, I'll notify the movers. They'll find them." He was trying to reassure himself as much as me. "Just remember, your poems are registered with our Toronto lawyer, so if they don't show up, we'll contact him."

Week after week the calls were made to the moving company. Months passed. My frustration level grew. Over and over we were told, "We're searching for your boxes, they're bound to show up somewhere."

I had planned to spend time putting my poems together for publication after the move. Now I had nothing to work with. I alternated between being angry and being totally frustrated. When I sat down to compose, nothing came. It was a devastating loss to me personally. Paul felt the pain of my loss, and sorrowed about this as well, but it was difficult for him to fully comprehend what I was feeling, even though he had lost things that were important to him too. Besides, he was busy with his new work and was on the road much of the time. His was a big responsibility.

By the end of that first year in Vancouver, the moving company was out of business. By 1982, we still hadn't been able to track down the lost cartons. Then we learned that the company had started up again in Toronto. More phone calls. Finally, we discovered the company had declared bankruptcy. We were at a dead end.

"God had his reasons for allowing this loss, Paul," I said as I sought to put meaning to what had happened. "Let's get on with our lives." And that's what we did.

Chapter Sixteen

The Infringers

Get rid of all bitterness, rage and anger. . . .

Ephesians 4: 31

In 1983, Paul and I took our daughters with us to Holland for the Conference of Itinerant Evangelists, hosted by the Billy Graham Evangelistic Association. Passing through the state of Washington on our way home, we came across a calligraphy of the "Footprints" poem in a Christian bookstore. I was dumbfounded. To say we were shocked is to put it mildly.

We purchased the plaque to compare it with my poem, which, of course, I had committed to memory and had since written down.

We found it to be very, very close to the original wording. The woman purporting to be the author had her name and address on the back of the plaque and I immediately wrote her. Her husband responded, stating that they would never steal anything and that we ought not to harass them.

Harassment? Surely this was not what we were doing. A simple letter of explanation was all I had written. Thus began a period of unbelievable stress.

Later, we went back to that bookstore and found a dozen other poems I had written, all done in calligraphy on plaques. I wrote the woman and her husband again. There was no response. After our repeated letters to this couple were returned to us unopened, we gave up the effort.

Several weeks later, when we were doing some ministry work on Vancouver Island, we came across the poem again in a bookstore in Victoria. This time it was entitled "I Had a Dream," the title I had given to the original version. The quality was beautiful. As we looked at the other plaques and bookmarks, we saw that they were now being published by a major U.S. publishing company.

Upon our return home, we hired a copyright lawyer in Vancouver. We had received the registration numbers of my poem collections from the Toronto lawyer. The Vancouver lawyer re-registered the material, and the publisher was written and provided with this information.

The publisher successfully skirted the problem by claiming to have a new manager who would be in touch with us. When she finally responded, it was to notify us that they weren't going to do anything about it unless they had proof of government registration on the "Footprints" poem itself. The lawyer had already sent them the registration numbers of the collections. It was an exercise in futility and only added to our growing frustration.

Wherever we turned, it seemed, we were bumping into the "Footprints" poem in one form or another. If it wasn't on cups, it was on plates. We found it on bookmarks and cards of every size and shape. Plaques, posters, calendars. You name it, there it was.

On a trip to Sebastopol, California, to attend a leadership conference, Paul and I drove to the pier in San Francisco for a break from the meetings. There we saw a man selling large hand-lettered posters, a new version of "Footprints." But this version was a paraphrase of the original, telling how he had walked with his friend on the beach, and how he had promised to be faithful to him, but his friend had died of AIDS.

We tried talking to the man on the pier but he became irate. "Everybody uses it, who cares, how do I know it's yours . . . ?"

Tears rolled down my face as I saw what a travesty this was of the beach walk Paul and I had experienced, and our conversation that had prompted the writing of "I Had a Dream" in 1964.

Later on that same trip, before leaving for home, we headed south from San Francisco to beautiful Carmel. We wanted to see the famous monastery there. To our shock, there in the bookstore was a picture of the Virgin Mary with a nun, and, in beautiful hand work, the story of "Footprints" from the vantage-point of a nun walking with the Virgin Mary. Once again, we left the bookstore, uncontrolled tears flooding from my eyes.

Another time, in another place, we saw a copy of the poem with someone walking with a child. It bothered me to realize how much liberty people were taking with something that had been so meaningful to Paul and me. One woman wrote a book, her auto-biography, in which she claimed God had given her the poem. She even had it set to music. I wrote her a letter. She did nothing to take it off the market; instead, she sent me an autographed copy of the sheet music. Then someone put it in a cross-stitch pattern. I wrote to them too. It made no difference.

People were making too much money off their products. We spent time and money trying to correct the situation, but it was fruitless, like going to a major fire with a handheld fire extinguisher.

More recently, while writing this, I've seen a version on handprints, a takeoff on "Footprints." We can see that something of the sacredness and specialness of the piece is being lost.

As Paul and I discussed what we saw happening, and as we prayed about this, we came to see that this was an infringement on something God had entrusted to me. We shared our concern with a doctor friend from Reno, Nevada, who said, "Look, I know a lawyer who has connections with a copyright lawyer in San Francisco. Maybe you need to talk to another lawyer. Perhaps it's time to look into this more extensively and see if there's something you should be doing to stop these infringements."

"Margie, we can't allow this to make us bitter," Paul cautioned. "We know what God says about that."

I had to agree with him. "I'm upset, Paul, not bitter," I assured him. "At least, I don't think I'm bitter. I'm frustrated, because I don't know what, if anything, we are to do. How are you supposed to handle a situation like this?" The question hung in the air. It required an answer.

We finally decided to have the San Francisco lawyer proceed with steps to ensure that the poem, now individually copyrighted under my name, was recognized, and that there would be no more infringements.

Chapter Seventeen

The Puzzle

See to it that no one misses the grace of God
and that no bitter root grows up to cause trouble. . . .

Hebrews 12:15

My aunt and my mother came to visit us right about the time we were agonizing over what to do about the "Footprints" poem. "It's like putting a giant puzzle together," I recall saying as I explained to them our dilemma.

In fact, at the time we had an extremely large puzzle on the dining-room table that I'd spent hours working on. I pointed to the puzzle as I talked to Mom and my aunt. "How are you doing with your puzzle?" Mom asked, as she nodded at the table.

"Well, sometimes it can drive you crazy," I replied, laughing. "Then I get up, go for a walk around the block, or I get to work. But I always keep going back!" My mother smiled knowingly.

"One of these days you'll have your answer," she wisely said, and this time she wasn't pointing to the puzzle.

Days later, after they were gone, I proudly exclaimed to the family that the puzzle was done. I had such a sense of satisfaction! It was beautiful. So beautiful, in fact, that Paul and Paula decided they'd put it on a board and have it mounted for the friends who had looked after our home while we were working in Australia and New Zealand. "Won't she be surprised!" they said to each other. And so, one day when I was gone for the day, they tackled the moving of it. They moved it very carefully, but suddenly the whole thing fell apart. To say they were absolutely beside themselves would be an understatement. They just didn't know how to handle it. *How would I handle it?* That was the big question!

I didn't handle it well. I felt outraged when I came back and discovered what had happened. Although I tried to conceal it, I felt angry for several weeks. But even worse, I could tell that I was feeling bitterness. Gradually it came to me that I had developed this bitterness in my life over a period of time, but I hadn't been able to admit it. Normally, a situation such as that with the puzzle wouldn't bother me. I would just laugh and say, "Let's start that puzzle again. This time you're all going to have to help!" and we'd laugh and joke about it.

But no, that wasn't what had happened. "I don't ever want to see that puzzle again, or have anything to do with it," I'd said as I stormed out of the room, crying.

It was our daughter Paula who lovingly confronted me. "Mom, you're bitter. Something's eating away at you. You've got to get rid of it . . . ," and she opened the Bible. Putting her arm around me, she read from

Ephesians 4:30-31 and Hebrews 12:14-15: " . . . do not grieve the Holy Spirit of God. . . . Get rid of all bitterness, rage and anger. . . . Make every effort to live in peace with all men and to be holy. . . . See to it that . . . no bitter root grows up to cause trouble. . . ."

I thanked her for caring so much that she dared to tell me what I needed to hear. We hugged each other and cried together. Paula knew I was hurting deep inside. The episode with the puzzle was symptomatic of what was going on in my heart, and God gave her the wisdom to recognize it and then the courage to talk to me.

That began some soul-searching. *God, what do I do with the guilt that others should have? What is this bitterness that I'm experiencing? This anger? Why am I feeling so strongly about what's happened? I've tried never to let the sun go down on my wrath . . . I believe in settling matters. Help me, Lord. I need understanding and direction. I'm puzzled.*

Chapter Eighteen

Relinquishment

I sought the Lord, and He answered me. . . .

Psalm 34:4

*T*here was no audible voice, but God answered my cry for help.

I began to realize how difficult it had been for Paul to live with my frustration and pain for so many years. Even though our Little People's Ministry had taken hold and was growing, and we experienced the blessings of God on our lives, still, in my own heart, I carried a sense of profound loss about the poems—my life's work. After the conversation with Paula, it was as if God were unscrolling a part of my life that I'd kept hidden: *Bitterness, my child, is related to the people who are closest to you. They are the ones who feel the fallout from your emotions, your anger, and frustration.*

Your own daughter Tina, for instance, hasn't wanted anyone to know that you wrote the "Footprints" poem, or many others that she has seen in print. She's been very cautious not to let her friends at college know. Why, Margie, why? Bitterness hurts a lot of people. Your precious daughter is hurting because you are hurting. She doesn't fully understand her feelings, they are troubling to her, but it's what's happened to the poems that's hurting you, and so she doesn't want to admit that the poem is yours.

Bitterness is often based upon what someone has done to you. It may also have its roots in somebody else's sin, if you know about it and you feel they are getting away with something. But don't you know, Margie, that there is nothing hidden from Me? You've had a heavy burden on your heart for a long time. You've felt that you were being sinned against. I see your tender conscience. You do have a problem, however, and you need to let it go.

You haven't wanted to be rid of your dilemma. You've become accustomed to it.

Yes, I know, at times you feel things are going along just fine and you experience peace about it, but habits become binding, and they can strangle your personality. You are no longer the lighthearted girl Paul married. You, like a lot of bitter people, are bitter over something that happened many years ago.

Every time you go into a Christian bookstore you are confronted with your feelings. Try as you will to submerge them, they keep popping up to remind you. There is visible evidence in these stores to disturb you—you see evidences of "Footprints" everywhere you turn. You love these bookstores—some of the happiest years of your marriage were spent when you and Paul both worked in one in Toronto. Are you going to continue to allow these feelings to fester?

Margie, for seven years you've lived with this. You've done your best to write to people and to companies to explain the loss and the ownership of the poem. You've received many responses concerning it, but no one is willing to stop using it or publishing it, because it's making them a lot of money.

You've had one lawyer tell you to allow this to continue because it could work as a tremendous asset in your favor—a better reason for a lawsuit.

Dear child, I can see that you don't want this root of bitterness to keep springing up to cause you trouble. You do understand what I mean. You and Paul aren't mercenary—money isn't the object, it's not the reason for your feelings. I see into your heart. Here . . . here is peace of mind. . . . Take it, Margie. Forgive and forget. Let Me handle it. Let Me carry it for you.

No, I repeat, this was not audible, but spoken to my troubled heart. I knew what had to be done. I had to relinquish the pain, the right to feel angry, I had to let it go. All of it. It was stubborn, like a plant with roots that went down deep. If I was to experience that special grace of God and the peace of mind He promises to those who obey His Word and trust Him, then it was indisputably necessary for Margie Powers to take her hands off the reins of her life, to forgive and to forget.

By this time, there were two Canadian lawyers and two American copyright lawyers anxious to take up the case. Relinquishment would not come easy. Could I do it?

Chapter Nineteen

"Leave It There"

"Just leave it with the Lord,
The One you most adore,
He will bless and give sweet rest,
Just leave it with the Lord."

Thank God for the wonderful others He places in our lives.

"Mother . . . what do you think we should do?" I was making a long-distance call to my mother on November 25, 1987. She knew where we were, that we had to give the lawyers the green light to go ahead with a lawsuit, or put a stop to the whole thing.

"Well now, what would your father advise you? What would he have thought, Margie?" Dad had passed away ten years before, but we still thought of his good sense when we faced difficult decisions.

Of course, I knew what his answer would be, and told her so.

"You still have to make the decision, my dear," she said.

"Now they're saying we have to prove that the poem is mine, come up with an original copy of the poem. You know I can't provide that. . . ."

A pause, and then she made a profound statement. "Just a moment," she said, and I could tell she was thinking some more. "Your wedding book . . . what about your wedding material?"

"What do you mean, my 'wedding material'?"

"I'm sure you wrote some of those poems in your wedding album before you and Paul were married."

"Mother!" I gasped. "I did. Yes, I know I did. . . ."

It was as if the last piece of the puzzle had been found. I dropped the phone, ran to where I kept the wedding album, and there it was! "Mother, Mother, you're right! I've found it. Yes, I wrote it in our wedding book. It's here . . . it's here. . . ." I was jumping and shouting into the phone at the same time.

Both Paul and I had forgotten. We hadn't looked at the wedding album in years. Our lives were busy, the Little People's Ministry kept us on the move, we were parents with girls who understandably required a lot of our time and attention. Mother's words were as though just the right door had opened.

That was the day, too, that we discussed the decision that faced us with our dear friend "Uncle" Geoffrey Still, Canadian representative of Focus on the Family. "Go home, Margie," he said, "and write a three-verse piece for me, and I think you'll find great release and freedom about this situation."

"Uncle Geoff"—I fumbled for the right words to tell him—"I haven't been able to write for a long time. . . . It's like," and I paused, fumbling again.

"Go on," he encouraged me. "Like what?"

"Well, I facetiously call it 'The Great Brain Robbery,' but I just haven't been writing. And now we've actually found an original inside our wedding album. Does this mean we have the green light from God to continue? Oh, I'm so confused. . . ."

"She's right," Paul chimed in. "It's disturbed me for quite some time. Margie seems to have lost the enjoyment in writing that she used to have. She doesn't even write songs any more. And the fact that we've found an original copy in our wedding album . . . well, it does seem to cloud the issue. Actually, I thought we'd pretty much made up our minds to drop the lawsuit. Now this . . . I'm confused too."

"I don't think I'll ever be able to write again," I said sadly.

"No, no, that's not true," Uncle Geoff reassured me.

"I wouldn't even know where to start it if I did as you've suggested and tried to put my feelings in words on paper."

"Margie and Paul, it's time to put this whole matter into perspective. You need to answer this question: Will it have a negative effect on innocent people if you decide to pursue legal action? What about your ministry? Our choices always affect others. It's like throwing a pebble in a pond; there's a ripple effect. God has blessed the use of that poem worldwide. Will that be hindered? The most important consideration is: What does God require? What does the Bible say about such matters?"

Uncle Geoffrey was articulating what we'd discussed, but just hearing him say it did, indeed, put it in perspective.

"Margie," Uncle Geoff asked, "can you just leave it with the Lord?" The three of us looked at each other, the same thought dawning on us. "That's it," he said. "Go home, write your heart out, and call it 'Leave It There.'"

And that's what I did. In the early hours of the morning, I was awakened and an entire song with words and music came to me. I picked up my little flashlight on the nightstand, the pen and notepad, and scribbled out the words to three verses. I didn't even get out of bed. I was so tired, I fell right back to sleep.

That morning, upon arising, I remembered the incident. I carried the notepad with me to the kitchen table. It was like hieroglyphics. When I finally figured it out, after working at it until almost noon, I had the musical score in my head, as well as the words. And Uncle Geoff was right . . . writing did help me to sort out my feelings. I remembered the conversation I felt had taken place between God and me, I thought about my mother's words, I knew what my father would have said, I knew what the Bible said about taking Christian brothers to court, and I already knew how Paul felt. It was the right decision—I would leave it all with God.

Leave It There

Just leave it with the Lord,
The One you most adore,
He will bless and give sweet rest,
Just leave it with the Lord.

Just place it at His feet,
You know that He'll complete,
The work you've done has just begun,
Place your burden at His feet.

O Lord, I do delight in You,
And on Your care depend,
And know that as my trouble flees
You'll always be my Friend.

The words were based on 1 Peter 5:7. "Cast all your anxiety on Him because He cares for you."
The decision was made. There would be no lawsuit.

Chapter Twenty

The Peace of God

Make every effort to live in peace with all men. . . .

Hebrews 12:14

*E*veryone—Paul, our daughters, my mother, Geoffrey Still, and friends with whom we shared our decision—was relieved to learn we had decided against legal action. It was Geoffrey Still who suggested we write a letter to those whom we had contacted about the use of the poem. The letter was written and dated November 30, 1987:

> Pursuant to my letter [date], I want to make one final plea. I have been in touch with Mr.——, a copyright lawyer in San Francisco. His direction was to pursue legal action in order to protect my authorship of "I Had a Dream" and the various versions of that poem now distributed as "Footprints."
>
> As a Christian I have chosen not to take legal action. However, I once again request that all future printings of the poem "Footprints" show my authorship.
>
> I wrote the poem October 10, 1964. The original manuscript was lost in a move from Toronto

to Vancouver. "I Had a Dream" was republished in "Heart to Heart," a poetry collection under my name, in 1985 in Hamilton, Bermuda [which I had started to negotiate for publishing in February 1980]. Just recently, an original copy of the poem was discovered.

In 1987, Hallmark Cards asked for rights to use "Footprints" and the poem "Letter from a Friend." The other companies who have use of the poems are: Knight Editorial Services, Antioch, Tennessee; the C. M. Paula Company, Cincinnati, Ohio; Majesty Music, Greenville, South Carolina; and One Way Street Puppet Ministry, Littleton, Colorado.

Today I can walk into any bookstore and try to feel comfortable about the decision that was made. I am no longer bitter that others have used my work, even though I don't like some of the adaptations they have made for their own purposes. I have learned to forgive and forget as the Lord has gently nudged me along to more important things. And in setting aside my feelings of ownership to these words that God put into my heart, I have at last escaped the frustrations that were making my life—and my family's life—so difficult. I feel I have recovered my wholeness of heart. That's what the peace of God does for you.

The trials that we have had recently—Paula's terrible fall at Golden Ears Park, and Paul's heart attack—have reminded me that we must save our strength and will to live our lives to God's purposes, and not fritter them away on personal grievances. My family and I are at peace again, after difficult times. Our work with children, the citizens of tomorrow, continues unhindered.

I am deeply moved when I hear accounts of what the poem "Footprints" has meant to someone. Following the 1990–91 Persian Gulf crisis, for instance, I read a newspaper account of a young self-effacing Marine from Tennessee who risked his life in an Iraqi mine-field. He miraculously survived. The next morning, the tankers and their crew studied the terrain, and found seven mines and some tripwires alongside his footprints. They told him he was either the stupidest or the luckiest Marine alive.

Lance-Corporal Mark Schrader told his buddies, and later the media, "I didn't see any tripwires!" Afterwards, squad members talked about the incident and someone mentioned the poem "Footprints." "It was obviously not my footprints that went through that minefield," the young hero maintains. "It was God. He carried me."

That story alone has made it all worthwhile.

It is my earnest prayer that the true story of "I Had a Dream" and the title by which it is most known, "Footprints," will have an even more God-blessed ministry in the days to come, as the reader sees how this very human writer struggled with her feelings, but how God lovingly carried her. What God has done for me, what He did for the young Marine, God will do for anyone who asks Him to walk with them through life.